perspectives
ON DESIGN
SOUTH FLORIDA

creative ideas shared by
leading design professionals

Published by

PANACHE
P A N A C H E   P A R T N E R S

Panache Partners, LLC
1424 Gables Court
Plano, TX 75075
469.246.6060
Fax: 469.246.6062
www.panache.com

Publishers: Brian G. Carabet and John A. Shand

Printed in Malaysia

Distributed by Independent Publishers Group
800.888.4741

PUBLISHER'S DATA

Perspectives on Design South Florida

Library of Congress Control Number: 2010930000

ISBN 13:   978-1-933415-62-8
ISBN 10:   1-933415-62-2

First Printing 2011

10 9 8 7 6 5 4 3 2 1

Right: Mosaicist, page 231

Previous Page: Howard F. Ostrout Jr. & Associates, page 197

Panache Partners, LLC is dedicated to the restoration and conservation of
the environment. Our books are manufactured with strict adherence to an
environmental management system in accordance with ISO 14001 standards,
including the use of paper from mills certified to derive their products from well-
managed forests. We are committed to continued investigation of alternative paper
products and environmentally responsible manufacturing processes to ensure the
preservation of our fragile planet.

perspectives
ON DESIGN
SOUTH FLORIDA

Tango Lighting, page 189

introduction

Howard F. Ostrout Jr. & Associates, page 197

Michael Wolk Design Associates, page 77

Creating the spaces in which we live and achieving the beauty we desire can be a daunting quest—a quest that is as diverse as each of our unique personalities. For some, it may be a serene, infinity-edge pool in the backyard, for others it may be an opulent marble entryway. Aspiring chefs may find a kitchen boasting the finest in technology their true sanctuary.

Perspectives on Design South Florida is a pictorial journey from conceptualizing your dream home to putting together the finishing touches, to creating an outdoor oasis. Alongside the phenomenal photography, you will have a rare insight to how these tastemakers achieve such works of art and be inspired by their personal perspectives on design.

Within these pages, the region's finest artisans will share their wisdom, experience, and talent. It is the collaboration between these visionaries and the outstanding pride and craftsmanship of the products showcased that together achieve the remarkable. Learn from leaders in the industry about the aesthetics of fine furnishings, how appropriate lighting can dramatically change the appearance of a room, or what is necessary to create a state-of-the-art home theater.

Whether your dream is to have a new home or one that has been redesigned to suit your lifestyle, *Perspectives on Design South Florida* will be both an enjoyable journey and a source of motivation.

concept + structure

elements of structure

contents

elements of design

living the elements

"Architecture allows us to be a part of a bigger whole; it creates those parts of culture that define who we are, how we spend our time, and how we think and grow."

—Brian Idle

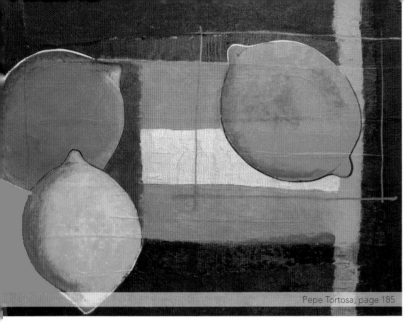

"Beauty is in the materials, the design, the craftsmanship."

—Claudio Faria

Genesis Automation, page 181

Dailey Janssen Architects, page 53

"Style is a reflection of life experiences; it changes with the times, people's expectations, and the structural demands of the project."

—Pepe Calderin

Aquatic Consultants, Inc., page 223

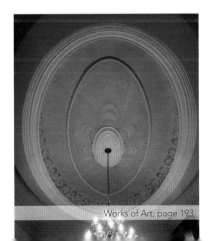

Works of Art, page 193

Architectural Form+Light, page 33

Village Architects, page 25

concept + structure

Fairfax, Sammons & Partners Architects,
page 59

New Architectura, page 65

Peacock + Lewis Architects and Planners,
page 71

Being artful, running a project efficiently, and building a home to last for generations need not be mutually exclusive. Onshore Construction & Development, led by principal Dan Reedy, is known for its ability to craft homes to exacting specifications, regardless of size, style, or site conditions. The team utilizes the latest Master Builder software to keep architects and owners apprised of progress and to keep the builders and artisans on track to reach the ultimate goal on time and within the initially established monetary parameters.

Onshore Construction is intentionally more involved in the creative process than most builders because it realizes that sharing its expertise regarding building techniques, material specification, and green technologies leads to smoother processes and better homes.

Taking exceptional pride in each of their luxury home commissions, Dan and his team of building professionals like to stay involved with projects even after they are complete. Because they know each home inside and out, they are well-suited to perform routine maintenance—and more than happy to do so—to keep the structure as pristine as the day it was built.

"The best projects attract the best people, and we wouldn't have it any other way."

—Dan Reedy

ONSHORE CONSTRUCTION & DEVELOPMENT

"By studying a site's solar and wind patterns, we can properly orient the home to capture light and breezes for sustainable indoor-outdoor living."

—Dennis Wedlick

ABOVE & PREVIOUS PAGES: Ideally located by the Loxahatchee River, the home is light and airy with virtually all spaces orienting outward. Clad in durable cedar shake siding, the exterior is accented by smooth white stucco details. A similar approach to contrast was taken for the interior: the Chippendale-style railing, glass and mahogany door, and plaster ceiling play off one another in the entryway, and the dark flooring and island balance the white cabinetry and ceiling in the kitchen. The great room is defined by the ceiling beams' gentle arc, which brings the space down to a human scale and draws your eye out to the water.

FACING PAGE TOP: We covered the terrace to provide much-needed shade while still taking advantage of the river's pleasant breeze. Roll-down screens offer additional protection from the elements and create a fully enclosed outdoor room as the occasion requires.

FACING PAGE BOTTOM: The master bedroom's ceiling detail is echoed on a smaller scale in the adjacent bathroom. Both spaces overlook the rear yard with pool, loggia, ipé wood dock, and river.
Photographs by C.J. Walker

TOP: New York-based architect Dennis Wedlick's concept for the Jupiter home is site-specific, eco-conscious, and an appealing blend of Florida modern and old Key West styles. We built the home to withstand hurricane-force wind and rain. Because the owners value an indoor-outdoor lifestyle, the multipurpose veranda became an important part of the property, for meditation and entertainment, children and adults, daytime and nighttime enjoyment.

BOTTOM: The second-floor master bedroom features windows on three sides, and views of towering banyans and palms give it a tree house, retreat-like ambience.

FACING PAGE TOP: Designed to capture rainwater for irrigation, landscaped with native, drought-tolerant plants, and outfitted with efficient fixtures, the home has staggeringly low water bills, eight times less than similarly sized new homes in the area. The same is true of electricity costs, thanks to passive ventilation, energy-saving appliances, and high-performance glass and insulation.

FACING PAGE BOTTOM: The kitchen and living room form the vertical axis of the home's T-shaped plan. We used renewable wood throughout: lyptus for the kitchen cabinetry and stairway, cypress for the ceilings, and cork to modify sound through the open-space plan. The other primary finishes—stone, tile, and low-VOC paint— are also green and bolster the air quality.

Photographs by Reto Guntli and Agi Simoes

ABOVE: Designed in the tradition of Mizner, the Tuscan-style estate on Jupiter Island embraces an unsymmetrical form that is interesting and authentic. The combination of half-round and elliptical openings creates visual interest.

FACING PAGE TOP: Reclaimed pecky cypress covers the entire ceiling, lending unmistakable Southern character to the entertainment area. The engaged columns were hand-carved of Dominican coral to define the openings of each archway. Because of the pool's vanishing-edge feature, swimmers feel intrinsically connected to the nearby Indian River estuary.

FACING PAGE BOTTOM: We installed the Jerusalem stone flooring in a random ashlar pattern to take advantage of the material's natural variations. The light-colored floors and Venetian plaster walls are punctuated by the stairway with mahogany treads and railing.

Photographs by C.J. Walker

Maintaining an intimate, connected firm at Village Architects takes priority for principal Deborah De Leon and partner Robert John. Seeking to work closely with everyone involved on the project, the principals have a holistic approach and pride themselves on designing both the interior and the exterior, down to the last architectural detail. The small, hands-on company gives them an edge over larger factory-style firms and allows for an exclusive level of customization.

Started in 1992, the firm began to develop a strong portfolio of single-family homes in response to the devastation of Hurricane Andrew. In the aftermath of the storm, Village Architects built up a strong clientele that has carried its reputation forward to this day. Focused on fresh new ideas and the most appropriate, cutting edge materials, the team pays close attention to a home's scale, proportion, and dimensions to achieve the right balance. Deborah has prioritized traveling, helping them gain insight, perspective, and inspiration from global influences. Extended trips to Bali have helped infuse water as an architectural element into the firm's work, giving new projects a reflective, clean quality that blends beautifully with the South Florida landscape.

"Home design is best kept simple, nothing over-the-top or pretentious."

—Robert John

VILLAGE ARCHITECTS

"An open-minded homeowner is one of the strongest assets to good design."

—Deborah S. De Leon

ABOVE & FACING PAGE: We used lush palm trees and Mediterranean landscaping to enhance a home's façade and add to the clean, classic look that the homeowners wanted. The cozy kitchen, den, and outdoor living rooms offer the family elegant island living with traditional beauty and timeless appeal.
Photographs by George Cott/Chroma Inc.

PREVIOUS PAGES: When we designed a vacation beach house for a family of six, we wanted to incorporate a strong Caribbean influence. The cantilevered wood wraparound balcony affords stunning waterfront views and accommodates the homeowners' family and friends, offering a casual island feel.
Photographs by Dana Bowden

RIGHT: We built the Key Villa on a distinct piece of land, offering a unique shape and a harmonious footprint. The sprawling shape of the lot worked well with the custom pool. The kitchen features well-crafted lighting for functionality while the open terrace offers a welcoming respite to enjoy Florida's ideal weather.
Photographs by Dana Bowden

FACING PAGE: We had to take extra care to make sure the vacation home worked with the irregular-shaped site. The pool and outdoor terrace offer waterfront views and take advantage of the lot's unique layout.
Photograph by Solo Photography

ABOVE & RIGHT: With water as an essential element and Balinese influences, we designed the house using modern aesthetic features, modeled after the pod-style homes. The courtyard entry and guest bathroom show off an elegant, clean concept. Floating in water, the breezeway and cabana structures stay true to the look of the Indonesian architecture.

FACING PAGE: Sitting between staff quarters and the garage space, the entry gate beautifully exemplifies Bali's modern style. We created the floating cabana to offer an outdoor space with pure elegance and allowed water to play a strong role in the home's architecture.
Photographs by Mark Roskams Photography

When a musician—accordionist, cellist, and bass guitarist—pursues pre-med, redirects into the accounting field, then fixates on Simon and Garfunkel's "So Long, Frank Lloyd Wright," his next career move makes perfect sense. With virtually no knowledge of the profession but a war chest of abilities and creative juices, Dan Carroll took up architecture school, absorbing its principles while mining his musical and biochemical foundations to then push its conceptual boundaries.

As the founder and principal of Architectural Form+Light, Dan has built his portfolio over the years remaining focused on his design philosophy, skirting notions of style in favor of innovations involving real-time problem-solving. Having worked in a variety of venues, he is acutely aware of how locale and personality affect the art of place-making. In the quest of developing thorough solutions, he approaches each residential project as an opportunity to express the essence of specific desires, at a specific time, in a specific place. This never fails to produce unique manifestations.

"Upon trying my hand at perspective drawing over a lunch break at my accounting office, my boss proclaimed that I could never be an architect. It was on!"

—Dan Carroll

ARCHITECTURAL FORM+LIGHT

ABOVE LEFT & MIDDLE: In the lady of the home's master bathroom, as well as throughout the Boca Raton estate, geometric themes of golden sections and extended circles and their compositional derivatives prevail. The vanity and other custom furnishings display these geometrical themes while providing requisite functionality. These motifs continue into the hallway, where groin-vaulting and distilled trimwork reveal meticulous attention to detail and proportion in both design and execution.
Photographs by Robert Brantley

ABOVE RIGHT: The owners have an interest in art that expresses the female form, typified in the wife's closet-cum-boutique. Frameless translucent glass doors and parapets combine with the concealed backlit translucent glass ceilings and minimal mahogany structure to render the space in an ethereal glaze. Drawers and shoe storage are built into the forms that reside beyond the chrome mannequin and her dog. Elsewhere, pull-out units conceal handbags and sports caps.
Photograph by Kim Sargent

FACING PAGE: A contemporary beamed ceiling offers comfortable scale to the living room, which frames sightlines across the pool terrace via a 15-part bow window composition. The water drop pendant, with its accompanying glass puddle atop the leather coffee table, is a tongue-in-cheek memorial to a challenging chapter of the construction phase. In the family room, a complex of layering elements modulates and enriches the continuous volume flowing into and throughout the adjacent kitchen.
Photographs by Robert Brantley

PREVIOUS PAGES: In the Long Lakes Estate project, the couple knew what they wanted but allowed me creative freedom. Guided by the site and the owners' need for a rather large footprint that was to feel intimate and belie its size, I developed the design to reflect their propensity for symmetry and their Boca Raton lifestyle as well as the South Florida climate. The front entry introduces the architectural themes, culminating in a cylindrical lantern supported by a massive cube of coquina from the Florida Keys, sheared to reveal the mahogany door. As windows are the portals into the soul of the dwelling, their effect cannot be overemphasized. Peetz Windows and Doors executed my designs with great precision. The rear of the house recapitulates these motifs as variations on their themes, enveloping the inhabitants in a courtyard defined by their architecture and the hypostyle of palms.
Photographs by Andy Frame

"Architecture is a bicameral composite. Building logic is left-brained; pure art is right. Both sides of the equation must be effectively juggled to achieve a responsible result."

—Dan Carroll

ABOVE: The Lighthouse Point project began on an airplane with the serendipitous phone number on the proverbial napkin. The family's coveted site rests where the Grand Canal and Intracoastal Waterway meet at an obtuse angle, necessitating investigation beyond predictable geometries. The resulting decagon is the residence's central generating element, and it manifests as a huge two-and-a-half-story great room with decagonal skylight and expansive views of the water. The room has hosted large events including the daughter's wedding and annual Christmas parties centered around a gargantuan tree replete with a choir caroling at the grand piano.

FACING PAGE: My concept for the challenging property was based on a central hinge flanked by two ratcheting subordinate wings that reference the adjoining waterways. Acknowledging the owners' love of Chinese art and culture and their many visits to Asia, Terracotta Warrior replicas guard the front entry. At one side, an I-shaped window frames the sculptural elevator massing perforated with art niches and presentations wrapped first in slate and then by a wooden stairway. The slate-clad grade level of the front elevation is completed by three double garage doors, each capped by a clerestory lantern of translucent glass over an ipé beam. These echo the focal lantern above the front entrance.

Photographs by Andy Frame

"The challenge is not so much in the composition of the primary spaces but rather in the interstitial transitions."

—Dan Carroll

ABOVE: In the kitchen, the great room's back bar, and throughout the home, televisions are equipped with the residents' personal aquarium channel, featuring live footage fed by underwater cameras recording fish society in the Intracoastal. Designed to cater to the residents' daily routines, the kitchen adjoins the breakfast room, which is outfitted with a sofa for socializing before and after meals.

FACING PAGE: During my initial interview with the owner, he announced "You're the one. You're the one who thinks outside of the box." I replied "Be careful what you say." Hence, eschewing walls, the home is comprised of boxes that float between columns. Each box's dimensions are identical but their forms morph in service to relevant programmatic requirements. The concept of the columns themselves grew out of the owner's desire to clear the site of several mature trees. Although it would have been compositionally convenient, I defended the trees' right to life. I told the owner that if the trees came down I would build them back. Alas, the great room is a decagonal composition of 10 two-story columns sprouting ipé and steel diagonal extensions that support an enormous Kalwall skylight and the roof canopy.

Photographs by Andy Frame

Whether working with homeowners to select the right team of architects, designers, and specialists or collaborating directly with industry professionals to realize their creative vision, ASR Custom Interiors' professionals are happy to lend their expertise. They are the ultimate researchers and problem solvers, helping everyone involved to understand what works, what doesn't, where to source the finest materials, and how to make the designs even better. Because ASR's construction management role means bringing together a vast number of people and pieces for each project, value engineering is a primary focus and decided specialty.

ASR's in-house staff is a few dozen strong but its family of experienced subcontractors and artisans is in the hundreds. This expansive network of trusted resources allows the firm to accomplish any look, be it a Zen-like haven, an Old World-inspired estate, a chic city loft, or a dreamy island retreat. Team members treat each project as if it were for their own family, and that level of detail attentiveness and care leads to relationships that last well beyond move-in day. As minor home maintenance elements arise, residents know that their friends at ASR will take care of them.

"Your home should delight your senses and reflect your sensibility. It's as simple as that."

—Cedrik Denain

ASR Custom Interiors

ABOVE & FACING PAGE BOTTOM: Using just a few exquisite materials in clever ways and impeccably lighting the scene can create a really memorable look, be it attention-grabbing or understated. It also ensures that the interior will keep people guessing when it was built for decades to come. Design by Bridgette Young.
Photographs by Gio Alma

FACING PAGE TOP: We were doing concealed cove lighting before the materials were even on the market. By constantly researching the trends and pushing the boundaries of what people think is possible, we hope to popularize many more design and construction techniques. Design by Levine Calderine & Associates.
Photographs by Barry Grossman

PREVIOUS PAGES: Drywall is one of the most challenging aspects of any project because it's so difficult to get perfect, especially where there are several layers and recesses, so we only use experienced craftsmen who can make drywall look like sculpture. For one room, designed by Levine Calderine & Associates, drywall was the canvas for a series of red glass mosaics—each piece individually installed. For another setting, it was the backdrop to incredible ocean views. However it's used, you know when it's done right.
Left photograph by Barry Grossman
Right photograph by Troy Campbell

"Perfection isn't a random phenomenon."

—Christina Shackleford

RIGHT: Our commercial commissions have given us a unique lens through which to view our residential projects. Whether we're working from the ground up, doing a total interior finish-out, or simply remodeling a small room, it all comes down to being attentive to the details so that wall to wall, floor to ceiling, everything fits so perfectly that you'd swear it was carved, not built.

Photograph by Troy Campbell

Aside from the beautiful surroundings and design-minded residents, one of the things Bob Mayer appreciates most about Florida's luxury home industry is how integral the builder is to every project. Since establishing Bomar Builders in the late 1980s, he has often been the first person that prospective homebuyers visit with, allowing him to utilize the depth of his skill set. From helping people determine where they want to live and how they want to be involved in the design of their home, to bringing together the absolute best architects and designers—including interior, landscape, pool and spa, hardscape, and lighting—Bob and his team have the ability to involve themselves every step of the process.

Primarily focused on custom residences, Bob enjoys the occasional speculative project, which gives him the opportunity to showcase his team's talent, think outside the box, be bolder than normal, implement tried-and-true materials in unexpected ways, and immerse himself in a variety of architectural vernaculars. When the task is to construct a home to someone's exact specifications, Bob notes that the three biggest things to consider are size, price, and level of quality, and he and his team can use any one of those requirements as a starting point for creative planning and value engineering.

"When you're building a dream home, the last thing on your mind is usually future resale value. That's where you rely on the expertise of your team to keep you dreaming big but grounded in making a great investment."

—Bob Mayer

BOMAR BUILDERS

"Extensive research during preconstruction and design phases helps eliminate surprises during construction."

—Bob Mayer

ABOVE, RIGHT & FACING PAGE: We've built homes that run the full gamut of architectural styles, including strict classical, Mediterranean, French, Palm Beach-Georgian, Bermuda, Plantation, contemporary, and modern. Having experience with so many different types of projects gives us an edge when it comes to catering to unusual requests and working within strict budgets and time frames. A key strength of our management team is assembling and creating relationships with the finest craftsmen and subcontractors in South Florida.
Above & facing page bottom photographs by Ed Butera, IBI Designs
Right & facing page top photographs by AA Marketing Group

PREVIOUS PAGES: The secret to making a grand estate feel intimate is creative massing, appropriate and contrasting material selections, and proper site utilization. These elements, combined with framing the architectural composition with correctly scaled landscaping, can soften and give warmth to even the largest properties.
Photograph by Ed Butera, IBI Designs

ABOVE & FACING PAGE: In a subtropical region where salt air, extreme temperatures, and humidity affect the longevity and maintenance of a home, we have established the best means and methods of construction to withstand the harsh environment. Owners appreciate the long-term minimized maintenance costs and their homes' ability to stand up to the elements.

Above photograph by Aero Dynamics

Facing page top & bottom right photographs by Ed Butera, IBI Designs

Facing page bottom left photograph by Corey Weiner, Red Square

Modern classicism is the Dailey Janssen signature. Distilling regional influences such as West Indies Colonial plantations, the Mediterranean villas of old Palm Beach, and architecture in the Florida vernacular, the firm creates unique buildings that respect the past yet embrace luxurious modern living.

While evoking the romance of their origins, the firm's traditional coastal residences remain rooted in the simple, pure geometry of classical architecture. Dailey Janssen Architects' focus is on custom, single-family homes, as well as minor additions and major renovations.

Led by Ed Dailey and Roger Janssen, the firm has grown since its 1990 inception, amassing an impressive portfolio that reveals a flawless attention to detail and a dedication to the art of architecture.

"With architecture, good design should always be the focus, regardless of style."

—Roger Janssen

DAILEY JANSSEN ARCHITECTS

"Classic homes can accommodate modern lives."
—Ed Dailey

ABOVE: We used sugar plantations in the western Antilles to provide inspiration for a perfectly proportioned villa with Dutch colonial details.

FACING PAGE: For us, modern classicism means adapting European architectural traditions to a tropical setting while accommodating contemporary lifestyles.

PREVIOUS PAGES LEFT: We always maintain a historical perspective. It's not our job to reinvent classical traditions, but rather to interpret them and elevate the meaning. Pure form and perfect geometry heighten the drama of the entryway staircase.

PREVIOUS PAGES RIGHT: Void of gauche features and showy details, our clear, concise work reveals the home's simple ornamentation.
Photographs by C.J. Walker

"Homeowners benefit when they've done their research and clearly understand everyone's role in the process of creating an elegant residence."

—Roger Janssen

LEFT: Outdoor spaces are often a family's favorite gathering spot in warm-weather climates. Volume, natural light, and attention to detail are as important for outdoor spaces as they are for indoor rooms.

FACING PAGE: We take any opportunity to blur the lines between indoors and out. Stone and wood appear on the interior while outside spaces offer luxurious comfort.
Photographs by C.J. Walker

Understated, elegant, and appropriate in every sense of the word, designs from Fairfax, Sammons, & Partners Architects reveal a multi-tiered approach. No single factor stands alone, and each element plays as critical of a role as the previous: culture, history, lifestyle, family specifics, and aesthetics inform the work. Anne Fairfax and Richard Sammons founded their firm in 1992 after collaborating with esteemed architects and firms worldwide. With the flagship office in Manhattan, the firm has also established itself in Charleston and Palm Beach.

Rooted in architectural tradition, the team begins with classic geometric proportions and a comprehensive understanding of the project, particularly the geographic dynamics of the site. Raised in Hawaii, Anne offers a keen perspective on harsh climates and their fundamental effects on a building's design. Fairfax & Sammons responds to South Florida's tropical climate in the traditional sense, often making beautiful use of overhanging eaves for water protection, large verandas for shade, and high ceilings that aid cross ventilation. The influences of England, Bermuda, and Italy make a strong appearance in the firm's work to reveal the region's rich architectural history. Neighborhood-appropriate and aesthetically pleasing, each house offers a certain comfort, subtleness, and grace—making it as much a part of the community as the family who inhabits it.

"Work classically, design regionally."
—Richard Sammons

FAIRFAX, SAMMONS & PARTNERS ARCHITECTS

> "Preconceived notions should be left behind when designing; the greatest possibilities come from an open mind."
> —Anne Fairfax

RIGHT: We designed a British Colonial, Caribbean-style villa on an exclusive resort in Jupiter that underwent a difficult endurance test during construction: gale force winds. Three hurricanes hit the coast, making certain that the durable, Bermuda roofs with stucco-covered tile held tight. Internal joinery with solid timbers of Brazilian cherry and mahogany add to the home's overall strength. Beautifully proportioned sash windows and crisp, white-painted stucco show off the clean lines of the house. Inside, the floorplan offers a natural flow, with the bottom floor circulation leading to the main living space.
Photographs by Allan Carlisle

FACING PAGE: What began as a John L. Volk home from the 1970s has turned into a modern Palm Beach estate. We maintained the original butterfly-like plan but completed extensive remodeling to suit the homeowners' tastes and lifestyle. The portico, front door, windows, and flanking wings were some of the areas we redesigned with classical detail. To create an airy, crisp setting with a touch of Colonial style, David Mlinaric and Hugh Henry used flowing silks, linen curtains, and soft hues.
Photographs by Durston Saylor

PREVIOUS PAGES: Our team was inspired by several styles for a perfectly sited Gulfstream home: Charleston Colonial, French Creole, and tropical British Colonial revival. In order to incorporate the homeowner's love of Thomas Jefferson's work, we included loggias, occuli, and corner porches that nod to Moticello, Poplar Forest, and the University of Virginia. Collaborating with Leta Austin Foster of Palm Beach for interior décor, we designed a guest bedroom in the shape of a half octagon with dado paneling and a tented, beadboard ceiling. Double verandas appear on the front exterior and add to the home's indoor-outdoor quality; Doric masonry columns provide a strong juxtaposition of positive and negative space. For the top-story veranda, we created a stunning light-and-shadow effect by using Chippendale-style railings that even Thomas Jefferson would appreciate.
Photographs by Durston Saylor

"Houses aren't commodities for buying and selling. Each is personal, lovable—a place where multiple generations may return."

—Richard Sammons

ABOVE: For a couple who loves art, architecture, and literature, we designed a suite of rooms to fit their interests. Smart, passionate, and elegant, each room suits the homeowners' academic hobbies without making the 5,000-square-foot apartment feel small. The Neo-classical influences dominate the library and entrance hall; the rotunda ceilings immediately draw the eye upward and offer depth and interest to the rooms.

FACING PAGE: Standing as a quintessential example of our take on regional Classicism, the Farmlands reveals the beauty of the American Federal style. Surrounded by 600 wooded acres, the house reveals meticulous craftsmanship within an architectural tradition that fits perfectly into the landscape. Carefully detailed millwork and Palladian windows with arched recesses typify Federal-style architecture.

Photographs by Durston Saylor

Architecture that evokes emotion is what Alberto Abad and Keith Martin of New Architectura bring to life through unique, contemporary design that remains timeless and expressive. Modernism and Mediterranean styles flavor the firm's architecture, planning, and interiors portfolio, but above all each home will be a tailor-made melding of the homeowner's and the architect's tastes for truly transcendent design that surpasses all conventions.

Founded in 1996, the firm is the realization of Alberto's dream to open his own company and be able to bring a greater modernism aesthetic to southwest Florida. His drive to become an architect dates back to middle school drafting classes when even his handwriting spelled out his future career. Education at the University of Florida and experience working for other firms have armed him with the ability to design a variety of homes, all imbued with an undeniable novelty. New Architectura creates always fresh, never routine homes that break cookie-cutter molds.

"We don't drive 1957 Chevys, so why build the same classic house from 20 years ago? The modern age we live in calls for housing updated accordingly."

—Alberto Abad

NEW ARCHITECTURA

ABOVE, LEFT & FACING PAGE: The North Carolina house brought in elements of mountain style to suit the setting. The Italian and English homeowner, fond of vibrant colors, wanted something unique: a palette of greens, browns, and black was essential. There were to be no steps on the main level of the house; however, the steep contour of the site made that difficult. We overcame the challenge; the home is two stories in the front but becomes three to four stories in the back. Cypress wood, cultured stone matching the local area stone, wood trim, and antique English furniture accomplish the required aesthetic. A very English billiard and bar area, decorated with golf accessories, suits the home's proximity to a golf course.

PREVIOUS PAGES: Facing Naples Bay, the all-glass home seamlessly opens up to views of the water. The first contemporary modern home in the neighborhood was a collaboration between the site, the view, and the homeowners—an interior designer and a closet architect. A center stair tower offers views immediately upon entry to the house.
Photographs by Tom Harper Photography

"I design a house for living. A home is not a home until it is lived in and you can partake of it."

—Alberto Abad

"I invest my energy in tailoring my homes to lifestyles, not to an arbitrary list of requirements. Each home is unique."

—Alberto Abad

ABOVE & FACING PAGE: The Villa Navona home reflects today's Mediterranean style: simple, authentic, classic, and elegant. Because Southwest Florida is perfect for outdoor living, the house's living areas freely transition from indoor to outdoor. The aim is to be as close to nature as possible. Each of our homes is geared for socialization, fostering gatherings anywhere in the home for a lifestyle of entertaining.

Photographs by Architectural and Interior Design Photography

With nearly half a century of history in the Palm Beach area, Peacock + Lewis Architects and Planners has helped shape the skyline by designing homes and buildings that provide structure to everyday activities. From the original founders to the second generation of ownership, the firm has supported community growth, creating timeless designs that meet the ever-changing demands of the buildings' inhabitants.

Infusing that history with new technologies and innovative techniques, the Peacock + Lewis team continues to base its philosophy in the community—helping the area define itself and realize its special nuances. The architects and interior designers apply a close analysis of the site, the current conditions, and the potential to reuse materials or portions of a building, then consider the costs as if it were their own financial resources being used. Once design is under way, spatial relationships, volumes, and proportions are analyzed and developed to achieve the most effective, efficient, and exciting spaces.

With inspiration from Winston Churchill, who said, "We shape our buildings; thereafter they shape us," the designers at Peacock + Lewis strive to create stimulating spaces that inspire people to feel good about where they live, work, and recreate.

"Architecture allows us to be a part of a bigger whole; it creates those parts of culture that define who we are, how we spend our time, and how we think and grow."

—Brian Idle

PEACOCK + LEWIS ARCHITECTS AND PLANNERS

"One home at a time, one building at a time, architecture builds the fabric of community."

—Jon Olson

ABOVE & FACING PAGE: During a redesign for a family of golfers, we incorporated numerous energy efficient concepts, including maximizing the natural sunlight with views to the golf course so that virtually no artificial light is needed in the living areas during the day. Large operable windows in conjunction with ceiling fans allow prevailing breezes to cool the home when the humidity is low. Large potted palms, light-toned walls, area rugs, and tongue-and-groove planked ceilings foster a warm, relaxed atmosphere.
Photographs by C.J. Walker

PREVIOUS PAGES: The renovations were intended to create the feeling of a Polynesian village that made sense of the disparate forms, as well as to appropriately highlight the homeowner's art collection. We allowed the architectural geometry of the residence to dictate a unique entry with soaring roof elements that lead the eye through the home to the Intracoastal Waterway.
Photographs by John Stillman Photography

"Vision is being able to take the variables and create a solution that results in a lifetime of satisfaction for everyone involved."

—Brian Idle

ABOVE & FACING PAGE: The development in Florida was originally influenced by John Volk, who set a precedent for island classical architecture. One of the primary goals of the new home was to integrate the homeowners' casual lifestyle into every room while maintaining a sophisticated feel. The first hint toward this goal arrives with the pedestrian-scale circle drive with a relaxing courtyard between the wings of the home. We maintained the traditional H-shaped floorplan to help segregate the social areas from the private areas. Light, bright interiors with custom millwork highlight the water and pool views. The bedrooms feature terraces facing the water, as well as tray ceilings and built-in breakfast bars and storage to maximize space.
Photographs by Scot Zimmerman

"Design is design, everything else is everything else."

—Michael Wolk

elements of structure

Imagine reaching a point in your career where everything feels effortless. You've perfected your art and honed your skills so completely that the work comes as second nature. Michael Wolk has found himself at that point after a lifetime as an ever-evolving artist. Wholly immersed in his work, Michael loses the rest of the world when he sits down to draw—he goes to a place where nothing else matters.

After attending New York's Pratt Institute, Michael brought his ideas to Miami and began Michael Wolk Design Associates. Amassing a team of top creative talent, the firm recognizes the critical role that furniture and interior design play in the world of aesthetics. Michael blurs the lines of furniture and art, and shows the intrinsic link through his designs. Long ago, European kings and queens embraced the importance of palace interiors and kept royal cabinetmakers and artisans in their courts, alongside painters, sculptors, and architects. Over the generations however, the craft of furniture making lost its place in the hierarchy of the arts. The team at Michael Wolk Design Associates brings that strong sense of artisanship and importance back to the trade, reminding people of just how much impact a chair, a table, or a room can have.

MICHAEL WOLK DESIGN ASSOCIATES

"You can't create objects with a life and a soul, they have to be made and that life and soul bred into them."

—Michael Wolk

ABOVE: The entryway to a beachside residence was somewhat contained. We opened it up and gave it a proper sense of scale.

ABOVE RIGHT: We designed a custom table and paired it with Brueton's Wolk chairs. The Swiss cheese ceiling adds interest and makes the space ideal for moon-gazing in the evening.

FACING PAGE: A his-and-hers bathroom meets every need imaginable. Two wash areas, a dressing space with built-in seating, a soaking tub, and 26 different faucets with hurricane-force water help keep the couple happy and offer a spa-like retreat.

PREVIOUS PAGES: A custom bed turned into a control center for a modern suite allows the homeowners to adjust everything according to their needs. We designed the footboard to hide a television and the drapery to open, while the glass shifts from frosted to clear—all at the touch of a button.
Photographs by Dan Forer

ABOVE & FACING PAGE TOP: We breathed new life into a Miami Beach apartment by removing a wall, reconfiguring all of the living spaces, and developing a sleek yet dramatic design. From the moment you walk through the front door, you're immediately drawn into the waterfront living room and enticed to lounge on the oversized sectional. Completely concealing unsightly media components, the custom console and floating shelves create a sculptural aesthetic.

FACING PAGE MIDDLE: I love square dining room tables because they have a wonderful sense of equality and intimacy and they have a nice contemporary vibe. Mixing chairs and banquette seating is a playful way to break from the expected and bring in a few additional colors and textures. I designed the chairs after the tufted leather look of classic car interiors and also painted the artwork that hangs behind the dining area.

FACING PAGE BOTTOM: The goal isn't to fill up a room; it's to select beautiful things and present them in a distilled, artful composition that is pleasing to the eye and soul. My design for the sectioned headboard subtly echoes the focal point of the room: the bay window facing the water.

Photographs by Carlos Domenech

"Ok is not ok, and good enough is never good enough."
—Michael Wolk

LEFT & FACING PAGE TOP: Convex on one side and concave on the other, the fireplace wall is a massive 14 feet wide and 8 feet deep, a true organizing element in the space. Primarily floored in limestone, a few sections of mahogany set key seating areas apart and give structure to the open layout.

FACING PAGE BOTTOM LEFT: Movingui wood cabinetry and absolute granite countertops define the Parisian-crafted kitchen, a residential counterpoint to the industrial design in Four Seasons Hotel New York.

FACING PAGE BOTTOM RIGHT: The powder room continues the home's minimalist, cosmopolitan style.
Photographs by Al Rickerts

"Furniture is not just a commodity; it's also an expression of what should be celebrated."

—Michael Wolk

RIGHT & FACING PAGE: Challenged to design the lobbies and other public spaces of neighboring luxury high-rise condo buildings, I knew it was important to give each its own character while still making them relate to one another. In both spaces, structural columns are dominant architectural elements; one is clad in leather and pierces the ceiling in the center, the other is veneered in wood and pierces the ceiling in an asymmetrical manner. Simple details like serpentine panels, concealed lighting, and warm seating vignettes further the distinguished look of both settings.
Photographs by Al Rickerts

"As Aristotle said, 'Quality is not an act, it is a habit.' We have a serious one and aren't looking to quit."

—Michael Wolk

ABOVE & FACING PAGE: The Trump organization gave us free rein for the interior of Trump Royale in Sunny Isles Beach. We wanted guests to feel totally transported and surrounded by water whether they were oceanside or inside. With a waterfall behind the reception desk, zero-edge ponds everywhere you look, cool ocean colors, a variety of textures, and natural materials, the design clearly references some of South Florida's most picturesque attributes: the sand, ocean, and sky.
Photographs by Dan Forer

PEETZ WINDOWS AND DOORS

Weston

"By actively participating in every phase of a project, nothing is left to chance."

—Chris Peetz

ABOVE & FACING PAGE: Since the 1920s, the Peetz family has engineered and crafted extremely high quality windows and doors. Today our work takes us around the world, but all of the manufacturing is still done in Germany, where precision is king. For a contemporary waterfront home designed by STA Architectural Group and built by East Coast Construction, with interiors by Pembroke and Ives, we fabricated and installed windows and doors for 25-foot-tall openings. For strength, there is steel structure; for architectural continuity, the frames are clad in mahogany. The scenic location definitely influenced the look: we designed narrow stiles and columns to allow for unobstructed views and to adhere to the contemporary vernacular.
Photographs by Robert Brantley Photography

"Having the skills and tools to unleash an architect's creative potential is a powerful thing."

—Eva Leon

LEFT: All of our pieces are personally designed, manufactured, and installed by our artisans, so we are capable of developing very complex windows, doors, and façade systems. Once we understand the project's parameters, we do shop drawings, develop the plans, and submit profile samples to the architect and homeowner so that everyone is confident about the aesthetic. For one home, we brought the bronze cladding all the way up to the second floor for a sense of drama.

FACING PAGE: Z.W. Jarosz Architect and Holmes Newman + Partners' design was constructed primarily of stone, so the bronze entrance really pops against the creamy background. We developed special profiles for the front door, which features bronze clad to wood in a manner that promotes proper ventilation. A chemical patina lends instant richness and stateliness, and because of the piece's meticulous construction, maintenance requirements are minimal.
Photographs by Robert Brantley Photography

ABOVE & FACING PAGE: Sometimes speculative homes are the most breathtaking because the design team is constrained only by the site and the laws of the universe, not by an owner's programmatic or budgetary guidelines. For a spec project in Palm Beach, Dailey Janssen Architects and Addison Construction Corp. asked us to outfit the entire home in mahogany-framed windows and doors built to withstand hurricane-force winds. Whether single, French, sliding, or interior, our doors aren't merely built, they're crafted. Our team is full of experts who are continually developing new concepts and systems that push the boundaries of what is possible. *Photographs by Affordable Aerial Photography*

"It takes true artisans to successfully marry Old World traditions and cutting-edge techniques."

—Chris Peetz

ABOVE: Evocative of its Grand Cayman location, the island home is intrinsically connected to its beautiful natural surroundings. Our massive curtainwall system allows sunlight to infuse the interior. The home was designed by Cayman Style Architecture + Imagineering in collaboration with Marc Michaels Interior Design and built by Hadsphaltic International Limited.
Photograph by Insight Photography

FACING PAGE: When architecture, interior design, and construction come together in perfect harmony, a timeless aesthetic is sure to result. The collaboration of Architectural Form+Light, Alexandra Karram Interiors, and Prometheus Group for a sleek contemporary home made our task of outfitting the curvilinear structure with bespoke windows and doors a sheer delight. Many times, the exterior treatment is much different than interior, so we're really creating twice as many surfaces as the home reveals.
Photograph by Florida Design Inc. and Brantley Photography

ABOVE & FACING PAGE: We source wood from around the world in order to ensure impeccable quality but unless the aesthetic requires otherwise, mahogany is our strong recommendation because of its density and ruggedness. For a classical Palm Beach residence designed by Dailey Janssen Architects and built by Addison Construction Corp., we used mahogany with a painted finish for all of the windows and doors. Our proprietary lift and slide door system works well for the classically inspired estate but is equally appropriate in contemporary settings. Because it can be scaled up to a frame size of 40 feet wide and 11 feet high and the doors pocket right into the walls, the design possibilities are vast.

Photographs by Affordable Aerial Photography

"The best designed products read as simple and elegant, regardless of their complexity."

—Eva Leon

ABOVE & FACING PAGE: Embracing history in the tradition of Addison Mizner and other early architects of Palm Beach's great estates, Smith Architectural Group's design was built by Davis General Contracting Corp. The home's design places tremendous importance on symmetry, balance; the windows and doors are focal points of the entire composition, so developing the perfect profiles and executing them to perfection was as important as ever.
Photographs by Sargent Architectural Photography

"Marble, bronze, and iron are beautiful, luxurious, and eternal."
—Louis Beltran

ABOVE & FACING PAGE: As an architect, a designer, and an artist with a high European education, I contribute a unique perspective to each of our projects, at home and abroad. Metalwork may seem like a dramatic departure from designing buildings, but the transition was natural when I saw the need to bridge the gap between these disciplines. Early in my metalwork career, I was mentored by Parisian and Eastern European masters of the art. Two decades later, with my own workshop in Colombia, their influence is felt each time my team of artisans and I realize people's dreams using raw metal and ancient techniques. An Italian-American gentleman's coastal estate involved a great deal of planning and more than three years to create more than a hundred pieces of metalwork. In addition to dramatic front gates, a double staircase, balcony railings, doors, lighting fixtures, and various ornamental pieces, the estate has about 30 chandeliers, each designed to coordinate but feel unique, as if collected over a period of time. Inside and out, the metalwork is so integral to the design and aesthetic that you can't imagine the home without it.
Photographs by Alvaro Gutierrez

"Achievement means more than merely creating the metal; it means making the metal relate to the architecture and its occupants in a significant way."

—Louis Beltran

ABOVE: The residence's central hall was so gracious that our primary focus for the second-floor railings was developing a motif that would read well from afar yet be pleasing up close. Flowing between posts and finials in a floral form, the metalwork takes cues from the ceiling mural but neither element competes for your attention.

FACING PAGE: Metalwork is something that everyone seems to appreciate but few actually understand, so once we begin the design process and people realize the complexity of this art form, they get really into it. A number of homeowners and designers have visited our shop in Colombia so they can experience the smell of melting iron, the sounds of clanking, and the sight of strong, detail-oriented craftsmen shaping the metal. We have integrated a few modern technologies into our process but the majority is done with the same physicality as centuries ago. For large metal art pieces like staircases and gates, detailed site documents and engineering plans are provided to our craftsmen, who then manufacture the pieces in strategically planned sections for convenient shipping and installation. Our method is extremely efficient and ensures that the metal is married permanently and seamlessly to the architecture.
Photographs by Alvaro Gutierrez

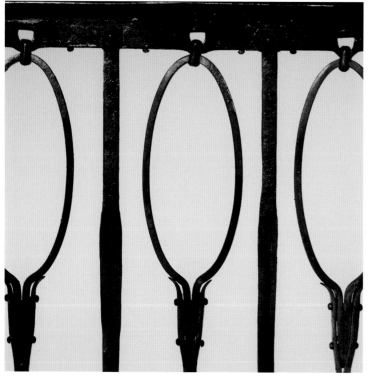

"Believing that everything is possible and being able to interpret people's dreams in this artistic medium are the greatest secrets we have to share."

—Louis Beltran

ABOVE & FACING PAGE: Because it is such an antique art form, metalwork tends to be associated primarily with classical, ornate buildings, but in fact it works perfectly with virtually any style, historic or modern. Metalwork is also a great way to reconcile aesthetics because while its form can be very contemporary, the manner in which it is created is always a celebration of materiality. When you observe it closely you can see the strength used to shape it and the rivets used to hold it together.
Photographs by Alvaro Gutierrez

ABOVE: Separating the dining room from the wine cellar is an 18-foot-wide by 20-foot-tall iron gate with an antique finish and partial gilding. The owner is extremely proud of the metalwork throughout his home and the gate is a true centerpiece when he entertains, which he frequently does for local charities. It's sad to think that in some parts of the world, where metalworkers are nowhere to be found, people seek incredible pieces of art and have to settle for something just because it's all that is available locally; at the same time, it inspires us to expand and bring our art and craft to every part of the globe so those dreams may be interpreted, developed, and realized. We're one of the largest operations in the world, but all of our work is wholly boutique, custom crafted, and we've been able to maintain that level of quality because of our passion and honed system for putting dreams on paper and then bringing them to life.

FACING PAGE: The raw metal comes to us in big sheets or heavy bars and is then cut, heated, bent, forged, hammered, and sculpted—an unbelievable transformation. Most of our large pieces are forged but we also have a complete foundry where boiling metal can be poured into custom molds made with wax, ceramic, and sand; it's an extremely enchanting and precise art process. The lighting fixtures were handmade with these techniques, outfitted with electrical components, and then finished with mica and stained glass. The large lantern, designed to reflect the gothic-Baroque architectural period, is about 450 pounds of handcrafted bronze.

Photographs by Alvaro Gutierrez

"The combination of natural elements and contemporary design creates a style that lasts forever."
—Murillo Schattan

ABOVE: In partnership with architect Patrícia Anastassiadis, we developed the vintage kitchen to really nourish the wellbeing of the chef, who in turn values the opportunity to entertain friends and loved ones. The furnishings' classic lines, sophisticated details, and exquisite color options are thoughtful and timeless.

FACING PAGE: The combination of contemporary design and a recycled wood-look finish gives the Satyrium kitchen a minimalist yet warm aesthetic. With lighting systems built into its modules and components, Satyrium's innovative and straight shapes demonstrate practicality. Traditional handles are replaced with post-modern features, giving a certain lightness to the cabinet profiles and maximizing the available space.
Photographs courtesy of Ornare

ABOVE: Built-in handles allow the smooth linearity of the Eria cabinet doors to shine. As with many of our designs, it was named after a varietal of orchid—a timeless flower whose form nods to our creative philosophy. Eria uses modern ideas in a format that is perfect for casual living. As beautiful as our designs for built-in and freestanding furniture are, the manner in which they're crafted is perhaps even more special. Because our company was established in the lushly forested country of Brazil, we are particularly driven to be eco-conscious in all that we do. Our craftsmen exclusively use FSC-certified wood and we work with a number of community outreach and recycling programs to ensure that extra trimmings are put to use.

FACING PAGE: True to our contemporary style, Satyrium embraces clean lines and strong forms but it also contains a bit of a futuristic flair: drawers and cupboards afford impressive organizational flexibility so that every plate, cookie sheet, and gadget has a place. Incorporating the dining table right beside the island confirms the concept that the kitchen is the heart of the home.
Photographs courtesy of Ornare

RIGHT: Just as the name implies, the Monograma line evokes the glamour and sophistication of days gone by through engraved metal handles. The design is intended for homeowners who appreciate fine details and fully customized spaces that enhance the pleasure of day-to-day routines.

FACING PAGE: Designed by Marcelo Rosenbaum, the Lite closet's dressing table with open shelves and gliding drawers is ideal both for people on the go and those who like to develop the perfect outfit for every occasion. Paint, neoprene, leather, and other finish options—from crisp white to vivid color—allow the closet to be as unique as the individual.

Photographs courtesy of Ornare

ABOVE: The timelessly appealing Art Deco movement—and all of its drama, geometry, and detailing—inspired the elegant Manhattan bathroom design. In collaboration with Patrícia Anastassiadis, we developed Manhattan to appear equally pleasing in a finish of matte or glossy, colors ranging from white and platinum to coffee and black, and knobs and pulls of all sorts. With so much star power, it makes sense that the vanity is topped with marble.

LEFT: Mandarina is at its boldest with a striking high-gloss black finish and our proprietary Corian.

FACING PAGE TOP: Because our pieces are highly customizable and created by true artisans, we don't keep an inventory. Like our cabinetry and furnishings, each of our decorative Verbena vessels is made to order.

FACING PAGE BOTTOM: In Mirra, mirrored doors and Swarovski crystal-encrusted handles speak to the modern woman who desires to surround herself with luxury. Patrícia Anastassiadis' feminine touch is evident in the beautiful design.
Photographs courtesy of Ornare

"Beauty is in the materials,
the design, the craftsmanship."
—Claudio Faria

"Craftsmen have sawdust in their veins, and when that kind of passion is present in the creative process, it is clear in the quality of the finished product."

—Thomas Riley

ABOVE LEFT: The owners' grandchildren's initials are routed into the panels of the walnut partition for a personalized touch. The vanity is solid cypress with the sink bowl and top carved from one solid cypress log to create a cohesive, crafted look.

ABOVE RIGHT: The main hall has two identical corridors with cased openings cascading to a paneled art niche. We fabricated the eggplant-colored pedestal with a thick polished acrylic top to support the antique urn.

FACING PAGE: A king-sized Murphy bed and storage cabinets are perfectly concealed within the steamed European beech veneer wall. Adjusting the Murphy hardware to allow the bed panels to stay flush and operate smoothly was a painstaking challenge requiring patience and determination.
Photographs by Sargent Architectural Photography

"Implementing complex projects requires meticulous attention to every detail."

—Douglas Poe

ABOVE: With walls spanning 30 feet and a gracious 14-foot-high coffered ceiling, the great room is elegantly appointed with English brown oak solids and veneers with white oak burl accents. The bar's hand-carved brackets and the chair rail's hand-carved egg-and-dart wainscoting cap are finishing touches that bring the space to life.

FACING PAGE: The dining room cabinets are curved to follow the radius of the floor pattern, and small bookcases between the windows provide visual continuity. Curved work is highly labor-intensive, requiring multiple laminations of thin layers of wood built up to achieve the final thickness. These pieces feature a multi-color painted and glazed finish with gilded accents. The curvature of the room is highlighted by the stained cypress ceiling beams.
Photographs by Sargent Architectural Photography

"Essentially, an artisan is a sharp tool that makes the design team's dreams possible."

—Benjamin Riley

ABOVE: Complementary to the home's classical décor, we gave the built-in bar an ornamental furniture base, so it looks more like a freestanding antique than a permanent fixture. The heirloom-quality piece is made of American black walnut with crotch walnut veneered panels, finished in a French polish.
Photograph by Lori Hamilton Photography

ABOVE RIGHT: The long and narrow wine room showcases an extraordinary configuration of mahogany pilasters with custom, polished acrylic wine boxes mounted with custom brushed metal brackets. This combination of materials gives the space a contemporary and welcoming vibe.
Photograph by Sargent Architectural Photography

FACING PAGE TOP: Providing a grand sense of arrival to a penthouse apartment, the private lobby is clad in custom-stitched macassar ebony veneers. The main entry door is veneered in a starburst pattern of macassar ebony from the same tree as the walls. The sidelights feature backlit tiger onyx mounted in custom bronze frames.
Photograph by Sargent Architectural Photography

FACING PAGE BOTTOM: The kitchen area is brilliantly complex in its layout, functionality, architectural detailing, and millwork. A rich sensory experience is achieved through integrating a variety of techniques and materials, including wood, bronze, onyx, and stainless steel.
Photograph by Sargent Architectural Photography

"When an entire team shares a 'whatever it takes' attitude, great things can be accomplished."
—Matthew Riley

LEFT & FACING PAGE: The kitchen cabinetry is finished with a polished, high-gloss automotive white—a more labor-intensive process than painting a car. The adjacent bar area features silver-dyed ash veneer to complement the kitchen and coordinate with the metallic accents and abalone countertops. Modern design, when done well, is absolutely breathtaking. Because the clean lines leave no room for error, it's a style often undertaken exclusively by the most seasoned artisans.
Photographs by Sargent Architectural Photography

"Classic, contemporary, rustic—
wood flooring can fit any
specification and any style."
—Richard Dallett

ABOVE: An entire house received antique distressed flooring, which lent the perfect warmth to rooms like the library.

FACING PAGE: Though we're a small company with personal service, we work on a worldwide scope. Distressed long-length planks with a rich Tudor black stain achieve a warm rustic look for an installation in Europe. *Photographs courtesy of Bois Chamois*

"Vintage hardwood floors evoke an earlier era, but come to life through the best modern craftsmanship and expertise."
—Richard Dallett

ABOVE: Antique distressed wood is not limited to only traditional settings; it pairs surprisingly well with contemporary furniture also. In fact, many of our options land in modern homes, though rustic candlelight always plays off the beauty of the wood.
Photographs courtesy of Bois Chamois

FACING PAGE TOP: American Rosso floors, part of our contemporary antique line, add a truly fresh perspective.
Photograph courtesy of Bois Chamois

FACING PAGE BOTTOM: Architect Robert Dean designed a Tudor-style mansion in Connecticut with about 3,000 square feet of our flooring. To keep true to Tudor themes, he chose antique distressed long planks complemented by Versailles parquet panels—each component handmade in accordance with 300-year-old French tradition.
Photographs courtesy of Robert Dean Architects

OPUSTONE NATURAL STONE DISTRIBUTORS

Miami

"Nothing can replace the tactile quality and rich look of natural stone."

—Eric Schigiel

ABOVE & FACING PAGE: The detailed stonework of the motor court matches the scale and grandiosity of the estate. True to classical Italian style, the structure is supported by a symmetrical arrangement of archways and columns, accented with the ever-popular quatrefoil motif.
Photographs courtesy of Opustone Natural Stone Distributors

"Stone works equally well as a canvas and as a focal point."
—Eric Schigiel

RIGHT & FACING PAGE: Stone is appropriate for every surface: ceilings, walls, floors, and even freestanding elements. We import stone from around the world to ensure that we have the finest quality materials in the widest variety of veining and color palettes. The architecture's style plays a huge role in determining which type of stone will best achieve the desired look, but ultimately the material is so rich that it's nearly impossible to go wrong.
Right photograph © Antolini
Facing page photographs courtesy of Opustone Natural Stone Distributors

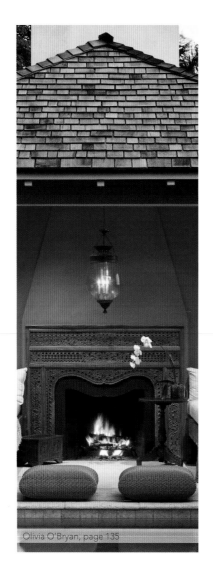

Olivia O'Bryan, page 135

Carlos Polo Interior and Lighting Design, page 143

elements of design

Jalan Jalan, page 155

Pepe Calderin Design, page 167

Tango Lighting, page 189

OLIVIA O'BRYAN

Vero Beach

"Detail-oriented on paper and laid-back in person—that's the best way to keep design projects both productive and fun."
—Ashley Waddell

ABOVE LEFT: The little girl's dressing room is like a jewel box. Because it's a cozy space, we could be quite bold with color and pattern, so we chose coral damask wallpaper, white accents, and an acrylic desk that allows the design to flow seamlessly down the wall.

ABOVE RIGHT: With ingenuity and patience, you can create just about any look, even without a huge budget. We wanted a sophisticated wall treatment to cover a broad space, so instead of commissioning ornate wallpaper, we specified an elegant, ordinary raffia and had it hand-stenciled. The aesthetic fosters an instant sense of warmth in the bedroom's sitting area and allowed us to choose furnishings with a playful quality.

FACING PAGE: Because of the living room's beautiful natural light, we wanted to keep the design soft and elegant. The combination of a stone fireplace, linen upholstery, white sheers, and botanical prints has a little bit of a Swedish feel: traditional but fresh.
Photographs by Jessica Klewicki, Big Blue Photography

"It's absolutely amazing how much you can do with a single fabric or color throughout an entire home."

—Courtney Whatley

ABOVE: For a couple who wanted to infuse their traditional home with contemporary style, we chose a crisp white backdrop and strategic punches of color. The wavy glass light fixture and ocean blue accents nod to the beachfront community setting.

FACING PAGE TOP: The concept of a banquette with multiple tables is perfect for avid entertainers because it's flexible to groups of varying sizes.

FACING PAGE BOTTOM: For a Caribbean feel, the owner specifically asked for dark tones, so we maximized the impact of light and color. We created a really tranquil environment by keeping the color palette soft and simple; the wood furnishings define the space without overpowering it.
Photographs by Jessica Klewicki, Big Blue Photography

"There are so many surprises and changes that take place during each design project that you just have to stay focused and keep a positive attitude; when you trust yourself and care about quality, everything comes together."
—Ashley Waddell

ABOVE: We chose oversized chairs with a dramatic navy and white stripe to match the scale and drama of the pool terrace.

RIGHT: Outdoor draperies are a great way to add softness without detracting from the scenery. By complementing the architecture with a few key Balinese accents and antique beds that serve as lounge seating, we struck the perfect balance between elegance and simplicity.

FACING PAGE TOP: We enhanced the contemporary-style living room by mixing expressive nude sketches with the chrome detailed fireplace. The most distilled designs truly are the best because they're relaxing and invite you to linger.

FACING PAGE BOTTOM: The whole design began with the fabulous wood and stone coffee table, a piece that the owners fell in love with and we were thrilled to work with. It's a strong enough element and the architecture is so impeccable that the room really didn't require any sort of dramatic pattern to hold your interest. The living room is a wonderful place to enjoy a quiet moment and gaze out at the gardens.

Photographs by Jessica Klewicki, Big Blue Photography

"We like to keep things simple, not overly 'decorated,' so the home feels like home."

—Courtney Whatley

ABOVE: Designing globally inspired living spaces can be tricky because you want them to feel authentic yet refined and livable. When a couple requested Moroccan flair, we decided that a departure from the norm would be necessary to set the right vibe. Instead of typical nightstands, we ran an extra-long console behind the king-size bed. We added an oversized metal mirror to dramatically bring nature indoors.

ABOVE RIGHT: Our design for the loggia is intentionally simple, allowing beautiful artifacts to be the defining focal points. The weathered teak cabinet establishes an international look and doubles as towel storage. When we shop for others, we'll only acquire pieces that we love enough to have for ourselves; it's a checkpoint that keeps the design beautifully cohesive.

FACING PAGE: Perfectly framed by the contrasting ocher and deep orange walls, the fireplace is designed around an antique Balinese wedding bed panel. We manipulated the poolside lounge area's small size to create a very warm and embracing ambience, replete with antique daybeds and a spectacular antique light fixture.

Photographs by Jessica Klewicki, Big Blue Photography

CARLOS POLO INTERIOR AND LIGHTING DESIGN

Miami—Tampa Bay

"The art of interior design is being able to visualize a space's full potential, whether the existing style needs to be completely reinterpreted or the architecture doesn't even exist yet."
—Carlos Polo

ABOVE & FACING PAGE: I completely redesigned the estate home to reflect the new owners' more contemporary tastes. The French stone flooring and quartz fireplace wall form a fresh canvas for the modern Italian furnishings by Cassina. Perhaps the most successful part of the project is how well the forms, textures, and hues of the sofas, chairs, ottomans, and tables complement one another without being the least bit formulaic. Unique among contemporary spaces, the open living and dining areas feature a few elements of crown moulding, which unite the spaces and accentuate the height of the ceiling in a clean-lined manner. The interior design's Zen-like atmosphere is further enhanced by the strategic lighting plan. Adjustable, recessed halogen fixtures provide the bulk of the illumination, focusing on certain elements and letting others recede into the background. The featured lighting element is a beautiful glass chandelier from Murano, Italy—the form is a wonderful counterpoint to the paneled wave wall and linear buffet.

Photographs by Clark Duggar

"One of the most powerful combinations of design elements is fine art, luxurious furnishings, and thoughtful interior architecture."
—Carlos Polo

ABOVE: We reinvented a dark, '70s-style mountain home to be bright, fresh, and minimalistic. The new Zen-like space incorporates wood, stone, wool, and cotton as a reflection of the natural surroundings.
Photograph by Clark Duggar

ABOVE RIGHT: I love the clean lines of lacquer; the material is so simple, modern, and low-maintenance. In the master bathroom, I contrasted lacquer against dark stone flooring and a wall of warm metallic panels and framed mirrors to reinforce the minimalist look of the home.
Photograph by Frank Baptie

FACING PAGE: Believe it or not, the central wall that looks like water or flowing fabric is actually made of solid prefab panels. The design was inspired by one of the owners' fabulous sculptures. I love working with fine art, and the Hollywood, Florida, home had plenty of inspiration, most prominently the whimsical Alexander Caldor mobile. The contrast between this contemporary American piece and the formal elegance of the adjacent dining room keeps your eye totally engaged. Natural light from the new clerestory, recessed spotlighting for the art, and a pair of incandescent crystal chandeliers, which hang above the antique Italian dining table, complete the comprehensive lighting scheme.
Photographs by John Gertz

"I never pass up an opportunity to create a sculptural element in the heart of a building."
—Carlos Polo

TOP: I chose cabinetry made in Italy, stainless steel appliances, an island topped with black granite, and a floor of fine Spanish tile to create a dramatic effect that would draw people into the space. The open layout of the bar-like kitchen is great for enjoying a bowl of cereal alone or entertaining large groups of friends in style.
Photograph by Frank Baptie

BOTTOM: Originally, the home lacked character, with nothing but an ordinary wall separating the kitchen, dining room, and living space. To ensure that the new bar would look like it belongs, I designed interesting ceiling and floor detailing; it appears to rise from the ground and hover in space. The door at the back of the bar leads to a wine cellar that stretches all the way back to the kitchen. Halogen lighting creates the illusion of sparks in motion.
Photograph by Clark Dugger

FACING PAGE: I really focused on creating the shell of the space, playing with the planes of the ceiling, walls, floor—as well as the platforms beneath the fireplace and television—to develop a clean-lined yet interesting aesthetic. Then I complemented the interior architecture with a strong palette of materials and colors: oak flooring, stacked stone accent wall, multidimensional fabric chandeliers in the living room and kitchen, two different sofas placed back to back, a splashy orange ottoman, and a metal chandelier in the dining room. The painting at the far end of the space is an abstract of my cats; it's an unexpected touch that gives the room extra personality.
Photographs by Frank Baptie

"By keeping the atmosphere lighthearted and fun, I collaborate with homeowners to create warm, inviting homes."
—Cynthia Thomas

ABOVE & FACING PAGE: Because of my love for art history, I often weave in elements from other cultures and time periods to add interest and bring the home to life. For author James Patterson and his wife, I transformed a formal Colonial home into a more understated living space to better reflect the family's lifestyle. Pieces from many locales—a mirror from India, an antique chest from France, a teak British Colonial dining table—layer in eclectic touches to the design.
Photographs by Robert Brantley

"Creating homes that reflect the homeowners' tastes and sensibilities begins with their vision, which I make classic and timeless."

—Cynthia Thomas

ABOVE & FACING PAGE: The most exciting projects are new construction in which I am involved from the beginning. Collaborating with the team to create a home that is exactly what the homeowner envisioned is an amazing experience. Martha's Vineyard has a very traditional feel, so for a new home I crafted a classic, clean interior. I coordinated a lovely blue tone in nearly every room of the home and allowed patterns and textures to impart variety, including a subtle striated pattern on the dining room walls and a handmade blue and cream wool rug in the living room. For the loggia, a soothing green palette with latticework and wicker furniture generates a sophisticated cabana feel.

Photographs © Greg Premru

"A common thread should flow from one room to the other, weaving together the overall concept of color and composition."
—Cynthia Thomas

RIGHT & FACING PAGE: It's important to take advantage of every room in the home. By extending the kitchen into an adjacent sunroom, the family can relax and be together while the the kitchen is buzzing with activity. I captured the family's love of yellow, green, and blue to create a residence that breathed of elegant Palm Beach living. Bringing a sense of tranquility to the residence, nature is delicately infused throughout the home from the pineapple motif in the sunroom to the antique bird prints in the kitchen and living room.

Photographs by C.J. Walker

JALAN JALAN

"Ethnic chic is one of those rare looks that attracts just about everyone."
—Bruce Platt

ABOVE: Tables made from 3-million-year-old petrified wood, niche lines of contemporary European furniture that are difficult to find in America, tribal artifacts from remote Indonesian villages, original artwork, re-envisioned antiques—these are the types of elements that catch our interest. The pieces we acquire are one-of-a-kind, and since our inventory is constantly changing, coming up with displays is a real exercise in creativity. We identify a focal point, someone falls in love with it, and suddenly we get to reinvent the whole scene with the pieces we have on hand—cultures and eras are beautifully intermingled.

FACING PAGE: A tribal rug from Nepal grounds the room's composition so that the pair of LEE industry chairs can take center stage. Eco-sensitively made in the United States, the chairs are upholstered in exquisite textural antique rugs.
Photographs by Dana Hoff

"Wanting to be close
to nature and surround
ourselves with pure materials
is a very human need."
—Bruce Platt

LEFT: It's wonderful to see people focused on contemporary design get so excited about our international collection of accessories. Objets d'art like opera crowns from China, wedding jewelry handmade by women of the Hmong tribe, and woven North African hats with leather accents have a distinct, soulful quality.

FACING PAGE: The interesting weathered driftwood lamp is by Bleu Nature, a French design company with an unbelievable collection of environmentally inspired and aesthetically sensitive pieces. It's a beautiful complement to the fine art of Longstreet Collection—a collaboration between an American mother and son who are well-known for their handcrafted nature prints and photography.
Photographs by Dana Hoff

"Blurring cultural boundaries is a fresh way to come up with transformative looks."

—Bruce Platt

ABOVE: The richly patinaed African drums are a collection that has evolved over time as we find them in various remote destinations; by consolidating them to one location, we've opened up a world of possibilities for how they're displayed in the modern home.

FACING PAGE: We travel all over the world sourcing decorative treasures and work with natives to gather additional original handmade items and then consolidate shipments back to South Florida. Because all of the pieces are so unique, we know that once they leave our hands, we won't find anything exactly like them ever again; photographically documenting our finds for permanent archiving makes it easier to share. All of us—not just the formally trained interior designers who also create custom pieces—are really passionate about figuring out new ways to combine elements from different continents and periods of time to create new, sophisticated multicultural looks. A Moroccan rug from the High Atlas Mountains, a cabinet with Chinese fretwork, a Syrian chest with mother-of-pearl and bone inlay, wooden poufs from Indonesia, a bookmatched African walnut cube table—discovering such handcrafted pieces is our passion.
Photographs by Dana Hoff

Jennifer Stone and Dennis Jenkins Associates

Coral Gables

"I consider rhythm, balance, and color to be the most influential elements for an environment to enable a meaningful experience."
—Jennifer Stone

ABOVE: Low-slung furniture and the dark graceful piano ground the otherwise ethereal living room. Designed by Dennis Jenkins, the coffee table features a white onyx top that is somewhat translucent and sustains the sense of openness. We placed the furniture with respect to the window—to take full advantage of the view.

FACING PAGE: Designed by Dennis Jenkins, the maple-framed custom sofa features a curved back and sloping arms that quietly reinforce the simplicity of the architectural envelope. Maple boards behind the sofa provide strict horizontal lines, contrasting the sofa's gentle curves, which prevents the space from being too strict.
Photographs by Steven Brooke

"Inspiration comes directly from growing up in a tropical setting with a medley of cultures, cuisine, and color."

—Jennifer Stone

TOP: An expression of honesty, unstained mahogany cabinets and dining chairs present the true character of the wood itself. We hung chandeliers to contrast the strict right angles of the modern house, softening and warming the room, giving it a human element. Their seductive curves demurely hold their own against the strong linear articulation of the cabinetry, dining table, and window mullions.

MIDDLE: The beating heart of the home, the kitchen perfectly balances essential equipment and warmth of materials and hues. Colorful blown glass pendants contribute to the cheerful nature of the space. The single pendants above the island contrast the pendant with glass shades over the breakfast table, twisting and twirling with absolute abandon. Frank Gehry's "Hat Trick" chairs add a touch of whimsy.

BOTTOM: We used creamy vanilla fabrics with delicate gold patterns to complement the visible Jerusalem stone columns. Graceful bedside lamps provide a hint of sensuality to the linear quality of the space and distinguish themselves from the vertical impression of the columns. We positioned the bed to take advantage of the view over a small lake.

FACING PAGE: In the triangular-shaped entry foyer, the flooring of gold Jerusalem stone mirrors the shape of the tongue-and-groove fir ceiling. This volume expresses openness, which reinforces the transparency of the entry foyer and is a worthy introduction to the rest of the home. Upon entering, you can't help but to look up toward the astonishing ceiling, which is the equivalent of a church stained-glass window.

Photographs by Steven Brooke

"It takes imagination to propose an original idea; it takes courage to carry it through."

—Jennifer Stone

ABOVE: The dining hallway is an ideal example of rhythm, balance, and color harmonizing to create a meaningful experience. The bold colors presented in a dignified pattern of red and gold travertine and black granite bestow a stately approach to the formal dining room. The red walls extend the energy experienced in the hall into the dining area. Enjoyable, relaxed, and stimulating, the room is a vivid testimonial of color promoting the function of a space. According to Coco Chanel, an interior is a natural projection of the soul.

FACING PAGE TOP: The centerpiece of the enormous kitchen, a nine-foot-long island featuring an Australian verde fire granite countertop, allows for food preparation and social interaction. The natural woven roman shades introduce texture and translucency that soften the hard surfaces and reduce glare.

FACING PAGE BOTTOM: The tranquil color scheme of the Jerusalem stone floor continues on the walls, completely embracing the tub area. We used a neutral canvas for the bedroom that allows the dark wood bed to stand out. The fabric choices in shades of ruby, plum, and gold give the room a regal feel and provide equilibrium to the space with the careful combinations of color.
Photographs by Joseph LaPeyra

"Inspiration comes from the most uncommon sources and situations— be it travel, nature, or day-to-day experiences. There are no limits as to what will influence my approach."
—Pepe Calderin

ABOVE: A modern Miami residence features a grand wall beyond the banquet-sized table, catching the eye and showing off its rich detailing. The living room has neutral tones with a strong burst of color—the custom rug really brings the space together. Overall, the effect is a warm elegance that welcomes visitors.

FACING PAGE: For a foyer that needed a little more personality, we rerouted the ceiling. This heightened the space and let us create a floor-to-ceiling door with backlit frosted panels above, giving us the drama and character we wanted.
Photographs by Barry Grossman

"Style is a reflection of life experiences; it changes with the times, people's expectations, and the structural demands of the project."
—Pepe Calderin

ABOVE: Built for a tech-savvy media lover, an entertainment room perfectly fit the homeowner's taste. The room was designed with the 100-inch plasma television and distinct speakers in mind, among other cutting-edge electronics.

FACING PAGE TOP: For an inviting living room, everything revolves around an eco-friendly fireplace with an attention-grabbing mantel featuring backlit glass. Our keen design encourages upward sightlines; the cove ceiling illuminates the space perfectly and emphasizes its most attractive qualities.

FACING PAGE BOTTOM: A master suite should be the ultimate retreat, so we wanted to offer a soft, tranquil setting. The Peter Lik photograph offers harmony to achieve the ideal ambience. For the bathroom, it's all unbridled luxury. Dazzling mosaic tiles offer vibrancy and texture, playing off of the lavish infinity tub.

Photographs by Barry Grossman

"I love the beginning stages of the design process, when the ideas start to flow and a concept is solidified."

—Pepe Calderin

ABOVE: A distinct foyer makes a strong impression. We used wenge wood to create an undulating wall, with stainless steel poles and panels backlit by color kinetic lighting. Each element in the striking entryway is a work of art in its own right.

FACING PAGE TOP LEFT: Style and fun come together for a family room; we used stone, glass, and wood to create the perfect look for an entertainment space.

FACING PAGE TOP RIGHT: A steel infinity pool adds to the amazing setting on a rooftop terrace. The building's strong architecture and breathtaking views make the space memorable.

FACING PAGE BOTTOM LEFT: For a master bath, we incorporated exotic woods and precious stones into the custom designed walls, ceilings, and floors. An onyx fireplace serves as a partition between the bedroom and bath while offering its warmth and appeal.

FACING PAGE BOTTOM RIGHT: We aren't afraid of making bold statements. A Miami living room shows off various coffers and a central oval pattern that grabs the eye and gives the space a lively, dramatic feel.

Photographs by Barry Grossman

"It's not only about having the biggest movie screen and the loudest speakers. It's about enhancing your life and controlling every single aspect of your home at the touch of a button."
—David Frangioni

ABOVE: We love taking on unique projects—the more challenging the better. For that reason, homeowners who want something a little extra come to us. My team and I designed and built a state-of-the-art A/V system into a 1950s-style bowling alley with a soda fountain for the ultimate in-home escape. The Cadillac conceals subwoofers, while the soffit holds a projector that fires onto a drive-in movie screen for an authentic retro feel.

FACING PAGE: The theater goes beyond a home entertainment system and shows that going the extra mile pays off big. With a 2.35 CineCurve screen, Runco 3-chip D-Cinema projector, and 7.1 surround sound, the experience of watching a film is better than I've seen in any commercial theater.
Photographs by Myroslav Rosky

"When done right, home automation is extremely powerful yet simple to use."

—David Frangioni

TOP: A cover of every film in the owner's library is pictured on the video screen, to let the viewer easily make a selection via touch panel.
Photograph by Myroslav Rosky

BOTTOM: When we built a cutting-edge theater for a condominium, we needed complete isolation and seclusion from surrounding residences. We installed one of the first Steinway Model M in-wall speaker systems, digital 5.1 surround sound, and a 65-inch Runco plasma with digital processor. A touch panel controls the lighting, sound, automated shades, and television functions. Interiors by Steven G, Pompano Beach, Florida, designed the space.
Photograph by Myroslav Rosky

FACING PAGE TOP: For an engineer who needed a commercial studio and a personal workspace, we had to come up with a highly efficient, well-thought-out system. The room functions perfectly for unique day-to-day needs.
Photograph by Ken Nelson

FACING PAGE BOTTOM: Constantly working with state-of-the-art technology keeps us on the cutting-edge at all times. A 2.35 screen and the ultimate control panel changes the way homeowners watch movies—from a home theater to a cinema in the home.
Photograph by Myroslav Rosky

Dania Beach

"Bathing areas define personal tastes and lifestyles."
—Fatima Rodriguez

ABOVE & FACING PAGE: Involved in various aspects of the luxury lifestyle genre for nearly three decades, our family knows good design when we see it. Regular trips to Europe and exclusive relationships with all of the top manufacturers ensure that we're among the first to offer the newest, finest, most timeless kitchen and bath fixtures. One of the ways we set trends is by displaying imported designs before they've even passed code in the U.S., so by the time we're able to offer them for sale, people are eager to embrace the latest pieces, whether classically inspired or unexpectedly avant-garde. Burgbad's collection is exquisite, demonstrating the caliber of style you'd want from an Italian designer and the craftsmanship synonymous with a German maker. Whether seeking a sculptural tub that toes the line between traditional and modern, a sink with invisible drainage, or a complete suite of designer pieces—mirror, chandelier, tub, sink, and artful faucets—a well-designed bathroom can transcend its utilitarian fate and become a lounge for relaxation and meditation.
Photographs courtesy of Designer's Plumbing Studio

"Never underestimate the complexity of a bathroom. Ensuring the environment is perfect is as important as each fixture's aesthetics."

—Ronny Rodriguez

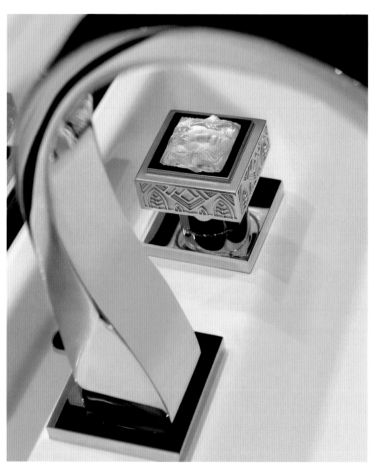

ABOVE: The handcrafted THG Masque de Femme collection combines a Lalique crystal bas-relief with enamel detailing and a chrome or gold base. Touching these exquisite works of art is a wonderful tactile experience, proving that every room—even powder rooms—are deserving of conversation pieces.

FACING PAGE: Gold and polished chrome have never coexisted as happily as in the black lacquer piece with sexy legs and a Swarovski crystal detail. Like a fine piece of jewelry, it is timeless and full of glamour.
Photographs courtesy of Designer's Plumbing Studio

GENESIS AUTOMATION

"Audio-video and automation design depends on the owner's lifestyle, as well as the look and feel of the home. Each project has its own unique personality."
—Valerie Law

ABOVE & FACING PAGE: We are the first company in Florida to use Crestron Systems to help achieve LEED certification in a large custom residence. The home has in-wall, remote, and desktop touch panels that monitor power consumption in the residence as well as control the lights, shades, air conditioning, pool jandy, cameras, security, and audio and video. The ability to set lighting scenes, make music playlists, check who's at the gate, and heat the hot tub is at the homeowner's fingertips. The option to set it once and forget about it is also available, with time-of-day settings and scheduled events, like dropping the shades in the afternoon to reduce glare and protect furniture or artwork. Homeowners can cool down the house before they get home or check the cameras from anywhere in the world. The control options are limitless.

Above photograph by Suzanne Barton, Suzanne Barton Photography
Facing page photograph by Ed Butera, IBI Design

"Homeowners can have sophisticated control with intuitive ease. No matter how complex the system or functions, it should be simple and straightforward to use."

—Valerie Law

ABOVE: When we designed a home theater, we wanted to achieve an elegant look without sacrificing any of the modern technology. The Art Nouveau theme with stained glass, rich carpeting, and velvet walls is equipped with the latest individually powered digital speaker system, a 2.35:1 aspect ratio self-masking screen, and a projector with Cinemascope lens. It's a 1920s glamour room that can shake the shingles off the roof.
Photograph by Suzanne Barton, Suzanne Barton Photography

FACING PAGE TOP: The master bedroom was designed for the view. The electronic systems were designed to make it versatile. Homeowners can close the shades for privacy, lift the hidden television when they want to watch, drop it when they don't, set the music before going out to the pool, or turn off all the lights before going to bed. Beauty meets functionality.
Photographs by Suzanne Barton, Suzanne Barton Photography

FACING PAGE BOTTOM: A chameleon room changes from a cozy den and pub room perfect for conversations to an incredible theater experience. With the press of a button, the curtains close, a projector drops from the ceiling, a screen lowers, and the lights dim.
Photographs by Ed Butera, IBI Design

> "Every day new light and shade, texture and color, stroke and line surprise me with fresh and delightful experiences and emotion."
>
> —Pepe Tortosa

ABOVE & FACING PAGE: Bright, strong colors are important in my designs and are influenced by my Venezuelan heritage. Growing up in a tropical country, I was surrounded by flowers, ocean, sky, and trees with bright sunlight; brilliant color was also found in the home and in architecture. My art often mimics this beautiful garden or natural environment with a magnified focus on a particular detail.
Photographs by Ronald Brohammer

"My paintings synthesize the visuals of nature, people, and animals that make up this world. This is my way of saying thank you to the creator of all this worldly beauty."

—Pepe Tortosa

ABOVE: I refer to my paintings as conceptual art because I play with nature in an imaginative way. Elements found in the natural world are incorporated in a unique design form—oranges and lemons painted with recessed epoxy glass windows or fruit involved in abstract designs, like a celestial combination.

FACING PAGE TOP: Portraits of family and friends, many painted with a focus on the eyes, led to the idea of painting a tribal mask with a scarification window to reflect people throughout the world who impose superficial scars on their body for decoration instead of tattoo.

FACING PAGE BOTTOM: In addition to color, texture is an integral part of any artist's design. I mostly paint on wood covered with gauze for durability and to exaggerate the texture of canvas.
Photographs by Ronald Brohammer

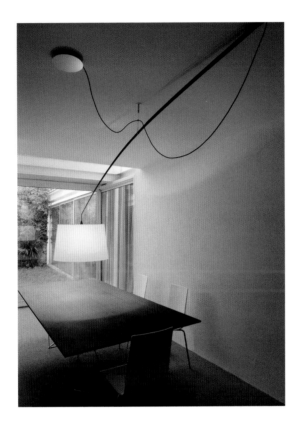 

"Scale, style, and functionality are the top three things you should consider when developing a lighting scheme."

—Jill Postlewaite

ABOVE LEFT & FACING PAGE: Born of designer Gabriel Teixidó's passion for fishing, Robin and Robinson were prototyped with minimal materials— fishing poles and wire—and aptly named after the great Robinson Caruso for the exploratory nature of their discovery.
Above left photograph by Jordi Canosa
Facing page photograph by Eva Gonzalez

ABOVE RIGHT: Nodding to the appealing line and form of 1950s lamps, the Nirvana table lamp is by Diogenes Paz, Catalan's Roberto Carpintero, and Gabriel Teixidó.
Photograph by Jordi Canosa

"The most inspiring designs embrace both contemporary style and classical form."

—Jill Postlewaite

ABOVE: Unlike the ornate designs usually associated with hand-blown glass, Mercer is a sleek, modern interpretation of lighting fixtures that graced ballrooms in the roaring '20s.

FACING PAGE TOP: Just as the name implies, Discoco is a clever take on the reflectivity of a disco ball. Modeled after flower petals, the opaque discs are made of fine quality injection-molded plastic and held together with aluminum rods.

FACING PAGE BOTTOM: In collaboration with Catalan's Joan Gaspar, Diogenes Paz designed Sophia, named after his newborn daughter. The delicate shape works well as a single focal point in a small room or as a bold statement of multiple fixtures in a large space.

Photographs courtesy of Tango Lighting

"Life is about creating things from your own unique perspective and then sharing them."

—Rita Stankus

ABOVE: As a child, my family owned several rental properties up north; between tenants my mother wanted to paint the walls white, but I insisted on something warmer and used the homes to explore color. Even today, I encourage people to simply pick up a paintbrush and try something new because experimenting with color is how you learn. Whether I'm designing art for a ceiling, wall, niche, or furniture, I take the same adventurous approach, use paints and materials of the highest, most healthful quality, and fine-tune the composition and its coloration to perfection.

FACING PAGE: In a single mural of an Italian countryside I connected the Lake Boca Raton home to its setting, brought lake views to the inland-facing side of the property, and created a visual reminder of the homeowners' passion for southern European living. The fixture below the mantelpiece is a source of hot water, and rather than trying to conceal it, I just designed the lake around it. The marbled backsplash and counter subtly meet the mural so the whole wall reads as one continuous scene.
Photographs by Works of Art

"Every surface is a potential canvas waiting to be imagined."

—Rita Stankus

TOP: The trompe l'oeil technique creates a wonderful illusion; even though you're looking straight at the wall, the streetscape appears to recede into the distance. A bear and a bull make cameo appearances outside of the New York Stock Exchange as playful references to the state of the market. Great care was taken to ensure proper proportions and alignment of painted architectural elements, both within the scene and in relation to the room. The other walls are faux finished in similar tones for continuity.

BOTTOM: Once the powder bath's walls had been covered with imported organic Venetian Plaster—composed of marble dust and lime paint—I stenciled medallions using nine different colors for a wonderfully layered look. Because there are so many values in the plaster and in the paint, the room feels very warm and authentic.

FACING PAGE: Inspired by an image she'd seen of Donatella Versace's home, the homeowner asked me to create a similar but even more complex, three-dimensional effect in the entryway. The center of the oval dome is faux painted to appear as fabric draping, and the outer circle is faux finished and layered with metallic paint and glazing. Because color has such a tremendous impact on how you feel in a space, it's imperative to get the shades and the look just right; the perfect hue will actually lower your heartbeat a touch and move you into a luxurious state of relaxation.

Photographs by Works of Art

"Each design needs to embody environmental sustainability, the homeowners' desires, outstanding aesthetics, and sublime functionality."

—Howard Ostrout

living the elements

The process of landscape design is not always as simple as it seems, but Howard Ostrout finds the challenge incredibly rewarding. Howard's years of experience, sterling credentials, referrals, and Harvard School of Design education help to explain his continued success in the field that he knew he wanted to pursue since he was a child living in Miami.

He is completely open-minded to all the possibilities of design and knows how to bring those ideas together with skill, knowledge, and a keen understanding of homeowners' wishes. With his listening ability and his vision at hand, he is able to draw out ideas with great thought and passion.

The artful blend of hardscape and landscape elements creates outdoor living spaces that look exquisite and simply feel good. Using innovative design features, Howard and his team of associates and outside contractors implement the multiple phases of each project to produce dramatic results. This process, in turn, helps to transform original concepts into extraordinary venues that will provide years of enjoyment.

HOWARD F. OSTROUT JR. & ASSOCIATES

ABOVE: Landscape architecture is essentially painting with water, sky, plants, hardscape elements, and light and knowing how to create the right contrast, depth, and scale. It is an exciting and fulfilling profession because with intense focus an elaborate project can be designed and constructed in a matter of months, and when it is finished it matures through the seasons and gets more beautiful over time. For a Jupiter Island home, I mixed a variety of exotic palms with hearty foxtail fern, which I love for its strong architectural quality. Landscape lighting adds to its drama at night.

FACING & PREVIOUS PAGES: Towering native coconut palms and fragrant frangipani trees form a tropical garden perimeter for the Intracoastal Waterway property. I specified the same kind of grass that is used for golf courses because I wanted a well-groomed look to complement the whimsical foliage. In the afternoon, the wispy palm fronds create fantastic shadows on the lawn and in the pool.

Photographs by Scott B. Smith Photography

"A narrow band along Florida's southeast and southwest coasts is subtropical, making the region conducive to a wide range of unique and wonderful plants that cannot be used anywhere else in the continental United States."

—Howard Ostrout

ABOVE: The large courtyard home occupies three lots in a prestigious North Palm Beach country club community, so I had plenty of square footage to work with. Mature trees, giant spider lilies, colorful crotons, hibiscus, and low shrubs figure prominently in the landscape design.

FACING PAGE: For a true sense of arrival, residents park in the motorcourt, walk through the arched structure—reminiscent of the charming bell towers that dot towns throughout Europe—and follow a nonlinear path that takes them through the garden, past the pool, and to their front door. Just a few moments' journey melts away the cares of the world. Architectural and landscape lighting makes the scene come alive at night.

Photographs by Scott B. Smith Photography

"Even small, transitional spaces offer the chance to create an amazing garden experience."
—Howard Ostrout

ABOVE & FACING PAGE BOTTOM: Lighted laminar water jets create perfect streams and puddles of color that instantly take the pool from a sunbather's paradise to a hip focal point for evening entertainment. Moving water of any sort instantly elevates the space from utilitarian to art that can be enjoyed day and night, inside and out. Opposite the spa is a circular onyx dance floor framed by rings of red onyx that are uplit by LEDs. Dozens of gas torchieres line a marble pathway that circumnavigates the property and leads to other sitting areas and points of interest. All of the outdoor features speak to the homeowner's playful and animated personality.

RIGHT: The Italian marble urns are three feet in diameter and positioning each required the strength of five men. I had them filled with red dragon-wing begonias, white angel-wing begonias, and dwarf ivy. When introducing bold color to a design, I'm careful to ensure that plants throughout the yard take turns flowering at different times of the year so that the palette is always interesting but never overwhelming.

FACING PAGE TOP: To give the entry passageway a garden feel, I specified a concrete base covered with smooth beach pebbles embedded into the mortar and then grouted.
Photographs by Scott B. Smith Photography

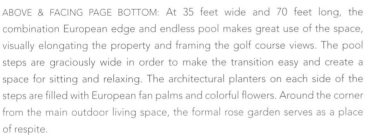

ABOVE & FACING PAGE BOTTOM: At 35 feet wide and 70 feet long, the combination European edge and endless pool makes great use of the space, visually elongating the property and framing the golf course views. The pool steps are graciously wide in order to make the transition easy and create a space for sitting and relaxing. The architectural planters on each side of the steps are filled with European fan palms and colorful flowers. Around the corner from the main outdoor living space, the formal rose garden serves as a place of respite.

FACING PAGE TOP: For the grand estate, I designed a motorcourt arrival area with a fountain and guest parking area for six vehicles. Clay brick paving was selected to enhance the classic architecture and reflect the colors of the clay roof tiles. The four majestic Sylvester date palms were collected from yards in South Florida; in order to ensure proper scale and immediate impact, the palms were chosen based on exacting specifications of size and height of the trunks and heads. In addition to sourcing locally grown trees, I partner with wonderful specialty nurseries and landscape contractors to test both native and exotic species and introduce new varieties of plants to the area, broadening my personal palette and keeping people interested and intrigued with what I will design next.

Photographs by Scott B. Smith Photography

"Outdoor living spaces must reflect the unique qualities of the site, environmental conditions, architectural style, and owner's personality and goals."

—Howard Ostrout

ABOVE: As part of an extreme renovation, I transformed an outdated pool into a European-style zero-edge pool and added wall fountains and iridescent glass tiles. To complement and frame the pool, I used about 20 different varieties of palm trees. Graceful areca palms enclose the deepest portion of the yard, and majestic foxtail palms are situated on either side of the pergola. On the side of the pool nearest the residence, pygmy date palms provide striking focal points. The richly layered view is enjoyed day and night from the family room.

FACING PAGE: The estate spans 30,000 square feet and the grounds are scaled to match its grandeur. An indoor gallery runs parallel to the motorcourt, so I used both ends of the deep loggia to create intimate plantings of holly topiaries and other delicate plants that echo the more significantly landscaped areas around the perimeter. From the front gate, through the front door, to the many outdoor vignettes throughout the four-acre property, every element of the landscape design works together to form a singular composition.
Photographs by Scott B. Smith Photography

BLUE WATER POOLS OF SOUTH FLORIDA

Miami

"Water is brutally honest. It's always perfectly level, so its vessel needs to be perfect too."
—Frank Vazquez

ABOVE: Cobalt blue iridescent glass tiles line the entire spa and pool. It's a luxurious effect that beautifully catches the light at all hours. As with any project, our goal was an easy, natural look. Getting to that point was anything but simple, though. Our exploratory work early-on prepared us for the structural components that would be required to make the pool a reality. About 25 pilings later, we had a solid foundation to ensure that the pool would be as structurally sound as it is aesthetically pleasing.

FACING PAGE: For an international rock star with impeccable taste, we collaborated with the architect before the home was even built to ensure that the mosaic glass pool and marble entertainment terrace would be a seamless extension of the interior living space. The elements truly look as though they were carved from the Key Biscayne island site. Our perimeter overflow pool is a feat of engineering and craftsmanship. Because the slit between the pool and terrace is just a fraction of an inch, the hand-crafted tile needed to be exactly aligned and level or there would be dry spots around the perimeter, totally negating the fluid effect.
Photographs by Frank Vazquez

RIGHT: My great grandfather was a famous Cuban architect, and there are several other architects, artists, and engineers in my family, so it's a privilege to be able to complement their legacy with a creative pursuit of my own. The opportunity to help people dream up a pool tailored to their personality and lifestyle inspires passion throughout the process. The more personal touches I get to add, the better. For a savvy businessman who wanted the flexibility to showcase works of art from his expansive collection during parties, I designed a small island at one end of the pool. It's an absolutely amazing setting to place a sculpture, elevating both the pool and the art to a new level. With a shallow bench following the entire perimeter, the pool is absolutely designed for the owner's style of entertaining—mingling in the water with a glass of wine in hand. All of the project's components—technical and aesthetic—are top-of-the-line, value-engineered, and installed by true artisans. Because I started out working "in the hole" just like my artisans, I fully appreciate their talent and the sheer strength and precision that the job requires.
Photograph by Frank Vazquez

"The best pools are extensions of the architecture and scenery surrounding them."

—Frank Vazquez

ABOVE: Truly a labor of love, creating the pool meant a mountain of paperwork, including securing permits from the city and an easement from the golf course. The result is just as the homeowner had dreamed: a contemporary sanctuary with beautiful views.

FACING PAGE: We used a black finish to give the new pool a rich, timeworn look, in keeping with the 1920s house and the historic Miami neighborhood of Morningside. Another way we made the pool really fit the setting was by bringing the lawn right up to the edge of the pool, a nod to classical styling. Of course even the most traditional settings deserve a little contemporary flair, and the stepping stones between the pool and spa nicely fill that need. As with all of our projects, the "pool coming soon" sign out front, which quickly changed to "now swimming," got quite the reaction from envious neighbors.
Photographs by Frank Vazquez

ABOVE: The lounge-like feel, complete with a bed platform in the middle of the pool and several around the perimeter, suits the owner's chic lifestyle. The most durable system, the most elaborate tiling, the most complex perimeter overflow design—everything is luxurious and pristine.

RIGHT & FACING PAGE BOTTOM LEFT: I always like to do something interesting with pool steps, because that's your first experience and it's where people end up spending the most time, believe it or not. The freeform design's oversized steps act as shelves for sunbathing, reading, enjoying a snack, or visiting with the swimmers. It's perfect for an active family.

FACING PAGE TOP: We often debate whether the focal point should be the spa or the pool. The truth is that it depends on the location and on what kind of look the homeowner wants. For the contemporary setting, it made sense to slightly elevate the spa area and give it a darker finish, punctuating the crisp line where the pool and terrace meet.

FACING PAGE BOTTOM RIGHT: We've actually had the opportunity to build two different pools on the same piece of property. The large, contemporary lap pool replaces a simpler Roman plunge pool, really expanding the backyard's visual appeal and usable space. Designing the new pool meant acquiring a 20-foot easement from the golf course, but clearly it was effort well spent.
Photographs by Frank Vazquez

"Enjoy nature comfortably in abundant shade."

—Dougan Clarke

ABOVE & FACING PAGE: Many of the greatest inventions arise quite simply: a need is recognized and then fulfilled. Our story of creating extremely durable, designer parasols, pavilions, and lounges is no different, but our mentality of continual conceptualization and development—from design and engineering to production—is something quite extraordinary. Exclusively made in Miami of the finest marine-grade metals and fabrics, our outdoor furnishings and shade elements are engineered to withstand the most demanding environments on earth. Our product line spans dozens of shapes, sizes, and unique styles in thousands of color and finish variations. With inspiration from a sailing vessel, our chic 16-foot Ocean Master MAX umbrella can be tailored to traditional tastes with our proprietary Aluma-Teak finish that looks identical to teak but doesn't require maintenance.

Above photograph by Dougan Clarke
Facing page photograph by Charlotte Hicks

"Rising in the east and setting in the west, the sun is a creature of habit. Taming the sun's warmth is a matter of placing your parasol in a solitary position where it will focus the shade and create an oasis of comfort where the shadow falls."

—Dougan Clarke

LEFT & FACING PAGE BOTTOM LEFT: Our commitment to being green extends beyond the manufacturing facilities; once our products find their way to homes or businesses, they stay there—unlike off-the-shelf products that are destined for landfills. A decade or two down the road and a few major storms later, our shade structure struts can be easily replaced thanks to our patented independent bracket system and solid mast and rigging systems. The Manta parasol design is a personal favorite because of its edgy look and its gentle curves that echo the graceful ocean flight of a manta ray. It embodies a wonderful balance in function and art.
Photographs by Rob Planken

FACING PAGE TOP & BOTTOM RIGHT: Complementing our Lounge, Pavilion, and Parasol collections, the Crescent reads as timeless yet innovative. Its sweeping arcs cascade to brilliantly polished trillion rib ends. Whereas the parasol opens from the center, the lounge and pavilion are supported from the outside, providing a seamless transition between the canopy and the earth. Because our lounges and pavilions are so well-constructed, lights, heaters, fans, misters, televisions, and speakers can be mounted right onto the structure for enjoyment day and night, all year long.
Top photograph by Dougan Clarke
Bottom right photograph by Andreas Seibold

ABOVE: The ultimate shade sculpture, the M1-Stingray is crafted with a fixed-shape canopy that swivels at its base to create a 360-degree shade platform.
Photograph by Andreas Seibold

FACING PAGE TOP: Our focus on enhancing outdoor experiences led to the development of our open-weave Air Lounge design. This new-millennium lounging platform is suspended between a spring stainless steel wave-shaped stand, which provides a gentle and luxurious ride into blissful relaxation.
Photograph by Marc Montocchio

FACING PAGE BOTTOM LEFT: When everything in a room—indoors or out—is impeccably designed except for one element, your eye naturally wonders what is missing. That was the inspiration for our Exuma design, which adds luxury to any exterior enclave. It can serve as a changing room, shower, storage area, or kids' playroom.
Photograph by Andreas Seibold

FACING PAGE BOTTOM RIGHT: Because every setting is unique and people's tastes are varied, our parasols are fully customizable. Before you think of the umbrella itself, determine the type of shade you want. The stand can be in the center or cantilevered from the side; the frame can be finished with several different treatments; the fabric types and colors are seemingly infinite; and the aesthetics range from classical to contemporary. Whether enjoyed on land or at sea, umbrellas are requisite to any outdoor retreat.
Photograph by Dougan Clarke

AQUATIC CONSULTANTS, INC.

Miami

"Water is such a fabulous medium. It transcends elevations, lifts spirits, and acts as a reflective surface for natural and architectural beauty."
—Brian Van Bower

ABOVE & FACING PAGE: The pool was designed to complement the size and shape of the modern home and the expansiveness and color of the sea without detracting from either. The vanishing-edge pool is cantilevered over the cliff for a dramatic effect and a strong connection to the picturesque natural surroundings. We chose to clad the whole pool in dark blue tile to create a surface that reflects the strong lines of Rangr Studio's architecture. Multiple levels of interactivity—from visually enjoying the pool as a water feature to sunbathing on the "floating" wood platform to being partially submerged on the shallow ledge, which runs the length of the pool, to swimming laps—makes the pool ideal for all seasons and occasions.

Photographs by M. Bouwmeester

"The architecture, landscape, and pool have to be totally integrated in order for the design to make sense."

—Brian Van Bower

ABOVE: To make the pool stand out against the vast ipé wood deck, we framed it with a two-foot bluestone border. Several unobtrusive umbrellas provide relief from the heat so that the pool can be used at all hours of the day. Creating such a meditative outdoor living space was not without its challenges. The island is composed of solid rock and part of the wood deck hovers over the ocean. Careful logistical planning, skillful excavation, and meticulous support structure construction were extremely important.

Photograph by Brian Van Bower

FACING PAGE: STA Architectural Group's design, evocative of the wonderfully natural dwellings of Bali, inspired the plan for the water elements: three sculptural vessels lined with translucent and iridescent tiles. The main pool looks the simplest but is the most complex, with its combination of a vanishing edge, a slot overflow, and an overhanging coping. It's divided from the shallow pool for children by a narrow walkway, which offers a "walking on water" type of experience before it transitions to steps leading down to the dock. Elevated a bit above both main pools is the spa—it is complemented by the perfect palm to shade the warmest part of the rear terrace. Our design of multiple pools creates a resort-like aesthetic, ideal for the waterfront setting and the island-style architecture.

Photographs by Matthew Pace

Miami

"Each pool is designed and built as if it were in our own backyard. A homeowner should enjoy the pool from inside the water and out."

—Henry Sanchez

ABOVE: A 20-foot-by-60-foot renovated pool features hand-crafted materials, including a glass bead finish with matching glass tile. The Tahiti Beach pool and spa overlook the bay.

FACING PAGE: The vanishing edge of the 16-foot-by-32-foot perimeter overflow pool allows it to appear to merge into Biscayne Bay seamlessly. The black absolute granite tile with black onyx pebble finish reflects the landscape and the skyline, while 10 synchronized underwater color LEDs provide vibrant illumination.
Photographs by Larry Sanchez

"From the tile and finish choices to the type of edge and any surrounding accoutrements, a pool should be a reflection of you and a natural extension of your home."

—Henry Sanchez

RIGHT: Built on pilings and designed to complement the architecture of the home, the 15-foot-by-40-foot newly constructed pool features handmade glass tile with a pebble finish. Sheer descent waterfalls flank a swim-up bar with underwater stools, while a vanishing edge connects sightlines directly to the bay.
Photographs by Larry Sanchez

FACING PAGE: A waterfront-edge pool in Miami Beach boasts all glass tile and ipé wood coping and decking. Built on pilings in collaboration with French designer Stéphane Parmentier, the 15-foot-by-30-foot new construction is a stunning and natural addition to the beachside property.
Photographs courtesy of Lux Productions

"There's nothing as luxurious as a pool clad in tesserae."

—Ray Corral

ABOVE & FACING PAGE: The tradition of mosaics began in cathedrals and palaces long ago, and while we still apply the same time-tested principles of artistry and craftsmanship, we have been able to branch out quite a bit from those roots. Indoor or outdoor, wall or floor, mosaics can take on so many forms. Our pool work ranges from simple monochromatic designs to ornate murals, and we orchestrate everything from conceptualization to fabrication to installation. Every piece of the creative and production process is absolutely crucial because when you're dealing with literally millions of pieces, there is no room for error. Our tile art is meant to outlast the architecture it's designed to complement.

Photographs courtesy of Mosaicist

"Whether they like classical or contemporary designs, people universally gravitate toward mosaics. Even as a seasoned mosaicist, I have to agree that there is definitely something magical about the medium."

—Ray Corral

LEFT & FACING PAGE: We can design, scale, and colorize literally anything to fit the look that homeowners want to achieve: a simple gradation framed by interesting borders, a dramatic motif right in the center, or a full ocean-scape with coral reefs, sea turtles, and fish designed to look three-dimensional. Our unique ability to take a project from start to finish with a team of in-house artists and artisans has given us an international reputation. If the installation is fairly straight-forward, we'll carefully ship our designs for installation by local craftsmen, but for the more complex we always insist on personally overseeing the project.

Photographs courtesy of Mosaicist

"Houses aren't commodities for buying and selling. Each is personal, lovable—a place where multiple generations may return."
—Richard Sammons

perspectives
ON DESIGN

SOUTH FLORIDA TEAM
ASSOCIATE PUBLISHER: Wendy Jeffcoat
GRAPHIC DESIGNER: Paul Strength
MANAGING EDITOR: Rosalie Z. Wilson
MANAGING PRODUCTION COORDINATOR: Kristy Randall
PRODUCTION COORDINATOR: Drea Williams

HEADQUARTERS TEAM
PUBLISHER: Brian G. Carabet
PUBLISHER: John A. Shand
EXECUTIVE PUBLISHER: Phil Reavis
PUBLICATION & CIRCULATION MANAGER: Lauren B. Castelli
SENIOR GRAPHIC DESIGNER: Emily A. Kattan
GRAPHIC DESIGNER: Lilian Oliveira
EDITOR: Anita M. Kasmar
EDITOR: Jennifer Nelson
EDITOR: Sarah Tangney
EDITOR: Lindsey Wilson
PRODUCTION COORDINATOR: London Nielsen
PROJECT COORDINATOR: Laura Greenwood
ADMINISTRATIVE COORDINATOR: Amanda Mathers
CLIENT SUPPORT COORDINATOR: Kelly Traina
ADMINISTRATIVE ASSISTANT: Tommie Runner

PANACHE PARTNERS, LLC
CORPORATE HEADQUARTERS
1424 Gables Court
Plano, TX 75075
469.246.6060
www.panache.com
www.panachedesign.com

TUUCI, page 217

index

THE PANACHE COLLECTION

CREATING SPECTACULAR PUBLICATIONS FOR DISCERNING READERS

Dream Homes Series

An Exclusive Showcase of the
Finest Architects, Designers and Builders

Carolinas
Chicago
Coastal California
Colorado
Deserts
Florida
Georgia
Los Angeles
Metro New York
Michigan
Minnesota
New England

New Jersey
Northern California
Ohio & Pennsylvania
Pacific Northwest
Philadelphia
South Florida
Southwest
Tennessee
Texas
Washington, D.C.

Spectacular Homes Series

An Exclusive Showcase of the Finest Interior Designers

California
Carolinas
Chicago
Colorado
Florida
Georgia
Heartland
London
Michigan
Minnesota
New England

Metro New York
Ohio & Pennsylvania
Pacific Northwest
Philadelphia
South Florida
Southwest
Tennessee
Texas
Toronto
Washington, D.C.
Western Canada

Perspectives on Design Series

Design Philosophies Expressed
by Leading Professionals

California
Carolinas
Chicago
Colorado
Florida
Georgia
Great Lakes
London

Minnesota
New England
New York
Pacific Northwest
South Florida
Southwest
Western Canada

Art of Celebration Series

Inspiration and Ideas from
Top Event Professionals

Chicago & the Greater Midwest
Colorado
Georgia
New England
New York
Northern California
South Florida
Southern California
Southern Style
Southwest
Toronto
Washington, D.C.

City by Design Series

An Architectural Perspective

Atlanta
Charlotte
Chicago
Dallas
Denver
Orlando
Phoenix
San Francisco
Texas

Spectacular Wineries Series

A Captivating Tour of Established,
Estate and Boutique Wineries

California's Central Coast
Napa Valley
New York
Sonoma County
Texas
Washington

Experience Series

The Most Interesting Attractions,
Hotels, Restaurants, and Shops

Boston
British Columbia
Chicago
Southern California
Twin Cities

Interiors Series

Leading Designers Reveal Their Most Brilliant Spaces

Colorado
Florida
Midwest
New York
Southeast

Spectacular Golf Series

An Exclusive Collection of Great Golf Holes

Colorado
Texas
Western Canada

Specialty Titles

The Finest in Unique Luxury Lifestyle Publications

21st Century Homes
Cloth and Culture: Couture Creations of Ruth E. Funk
Distinguished Inns of North America
Extraordinary Homes California
Geoffrey Bradfield Ex Arte
Into the Earth: A Wine Cave Renaissance
Shades of Green Tennessee
Spectacular Hotels
Spectacular Restaurants of Texas
Visions of Design
Southern California Weddings

PanacheDesign.com

Where the Design Industry's Finest Professionals
Gather, Share, and Inspire

PanacheDesign.com
overflows with innovative
ideas from leading
architects, builders, interior
designers, and other
specialists. A gallery of
design photographs and
library of advice-
oriented articles are
among the comprehensive
site's offerings.

Panache Books App

Inspiration at Your Fingertips

Download the Panache
Books app in the iTunes
Store to access select
Panache Partners
publications. Each book
offers inspiration at your
fingertips.

Panache Partners, LLC   1424 Gables Court   Plano, Texas 75075   469.246.6060   www.panache.com